WELL-DRIVEN NAILS

WELL-DRIVEN NAILS

HOW TO FIND CONTENTMENT
IN A DISAPPOINTING WORLD

Larry L. Lichtenwalter

REVIEW AND HERALD® PUBLISHING ASSOCIATION
HAGERSTOWN, MD 21740

The author assumes full responsibility for the accuracy of all
facts and quotations as cited in this book.

This book was
Edited by Gerald Wheeler
Copyedited by Jocelyn Fay and James Cavil
Designed by Willie Duke
Electronic make-up by Shirley M. Bolivar
Cover design by Willie Duke
Typeset: Usherwood Book 11/15

PRINTED IN U.S.A.

03 02 01 00 99   5 4 3 2 1

R&H Cataloging Service
Lichtenwalter, Larry Lee, 1950-
     Well-driven nails: how to find
contentment in a disappointing world.

     1. Bible. O.T. Ecclesiastes—Commentaries.
I. Title.

                    223.8

ISBN 0-8280-1361-6

With the prayer

that they will remember their

Creator in the days of their youth

this book is dedicated to my sons

Erich, Ehren, Ethan, and Evan

CONTENTS

Introduction
Thinking the Unthinkable

CHAPTER 1   **Been There. Done That. Now What?/17**
Ecclesiastes 1:1, 2; 12:8-11

CHAPTER 2   **57 Channels and Nothin's On/26**
Ecclesiastes 1:3-11

CHAPTER 3   **We'll Burn Our Skis for Uhler/34**
Ecclesiastes 2:1-11

CHAPTER 4   **Life Between Bookends—No Time outs/43**
Ecclesiastes 3:1-11

CHAPTER 5   **Wiring Your Brain for Eternity/53**
Ecclesiastes 1:13-18

CHAPTER 6   **When All You've Ever Wanted Isn't Enough/61**
Ecclesiastes 5:10-20

CHAPTER 7   **Honey, I Shrunk the Kids! No, It Was God!/73**
Ecclesiastes 5:1-7

CHAPTER 8   **Reality Bites and Ready-to-Wear Religion/82**
Ecclesiastes 5:1-7

CHAPTER 9   **Waxen Wings and the Neanderthal Child/90**
Ecclesiastes 3:16-22

CHAPTER 10   **My Fair Lady/101**
Ecclesiastes 7:27-29

C H A P T E R 11 Floating Lawn Chairs and the Happy Medium/112
Ecclesiastes 7:16-18

C H A P T E R 12 Have a Blast While You Last?/119
Ecclesiastes 9:4-10

C H A P T E R 13 Hello From Heaven! and the Necrophilic Romance/127
Ecclesiastes 9:5; Revelation 16:12-14

C H A P T E R 14 Birthday, Deathday, and the Scent of Your Name/139
Ecclesiastes 7:1-8

C H A P T E R 15 Dead Flies Floatin' in Your Tea/148
Ecclesiastes 10:1, 2

C H A P T E R 16 Unabomber, Solitaire, and *Cheers*/158
Ecclesiastes 4:7-12

C H A P T E R 17 Wire Walkers and the Ghost of Might-Have-Been/169
Ecclesiastes 11:1-6

C H A P T E R 18 Teddy Bears, Lollipops, and Olympic Gold/179
Ecclesiastes 11:9-12:1

C H A P T E R 19 A Last Nail for the Last Day/187
Ecclesiastes 12:8-14

Epilogue/198
Read This Book Again and Again

THINKING THE UNTHINKABLE

Fairy tales aren't supposed to end in tragedy. And great ships shouldn't sink on their maiden voyage. But the unthinkable does happen!

It happened when a black Mercedes carrying Princess Diana and her boyfriend Emad Mohamed (Dodi) al-Fayed careened into a concrete column in a Paris tunnel, killing all except a bodyguard. She was the most watched woman in the world. Many called her the people's princess, England's rose. She was young, beautiful, and royal, both a pop icon and a mother of future kings. When she married Prince Charles in 1981, Diana personified the fairy-tale version of royalty. Her wedding gown seemed to stretch the length of St. Paul's, and when the bridal couple chastely kissed afterward on the balcony of Buckingham Palace, millions thrilled to the spectacle. It was the opening scene of a grand 16-year soap opera that riveted imagination and hearts worldwide. Princess Di seemed to be the very essence of someone with a natural nobility that was classless. She appeared somehow to vicariously carry her (our?) mere humanity into the throne room.

When she died, her fairy-tale story was curtailed, and the outpouring of grief at her death was astonishing. More than a million people in central London lined the three-mile route of her funeral procession. Two thousand mourners inside Westminster Abbey attended her funeral service. They included glittering guests such as

Hillary Clinton, Elton John, Nicole Kidman, Tom Cruise, Steven Spielberg, and Luciano Pavarotti. Tens of thousands more gathered along roadsides to say farewell as her body was taken to Althorp, her family's ancestral home. And across the earth's 24 time zones, hundreds of millions interrupted their waking or sleeping schedule to gather around television sets. At Kensington Palace, where Diana had lived, grief literally mounted as bouquet after bouquet carpeted the lawn with a thick blanket of flowers. A global village was awash in sorrow.[1]

Elton John's vocal tribute touched the soul. England's rose was indeed a mere "candle in the wind." His words perfectly fit a life so bright, so vulnerable—and now gone. The grief at her death seemed out of proportion only if you forgot the real question it presented: "If the most luminous woman in the world can die, what hope is there for the rest of us?"[2] Fragile candles flickering in the wind—that's what we are.

The unthinkable also happened when the *Titanic* struck an iceberg in the frigid waters some 500 miles south of Newfoundland and sank within three hours. Just the human horror of the experience that fateful April night in 1912—during which more than half of the 2,200 on board perished because there were not enough lifeboats, during which the third-class passengers were locked below like animals and shot at when they tried making it to the boats, during which some of the richest people in the world perished with their treasures—is enough to haunt the imagination. "Even God can't sink this ship," the captain had boasted. But it sank anyway.

Ever since Robert Ballard found the *Titanic* in 1985 there's been a steady stream of books, articles, Internet sites, and movies about the depth of the folly that left this supposedly "unsinkable" British ship so vulnerable to disaster. And when James Cameron filmed the actual *Titanic* wreckage on the Atlantic ocean floor, he was inspired to make an epic movie as well. His was a *Titanic* vision—an epic Romeo and Juliet romance on a sinking ship, a forceful denunciation of wealth and power, a shrewd tirade on class snobbery, a haunting vision of unthinkable ghastly tragedy.

Determined to get his vision on screen exactly the way he wanted, Cameron promised to surrender his $8 million producer's fee and his share in profits. He resisted the pressure to cut back, and kept pushing and pushing the special effects, actors, camera crews, and costume people to the limit. The director built the biggest model of all—a 780-foot replica of the ship (90 percent to scale)—as close as possible to the real thing. He employed the exact shade of green on the leather chairs in the smoking lounge, and copied the design of lighting fixtures, china, and stained-glassed windows. In addition, he allowed no violation of historical truth. *Titanic* had the largest budget ever lavished on a Hollywood movie in the United States.

Cameron sought to transport viewers to another world, to enable them to catch the horror of the experience, to feel vividly the evil of wealth and power, to recoil at class snobbery, and to ache deeply because the sweet liberating love that *Titanic*'s heroes enjoyed for a few fleeting days ended in horrific tragedy and death. But most of all, he wanted viewers to leave utterly shaken. Shaken with the reality of human boasting and human vulnerability. His was a titanic imagination, and he wanted *Titanic* to stir moral and emotional imagination in a colossal way. He wanted his viewers to envision the unthinkable.[3]

Titanic became more than Cameron may have ever dreamed. It became an instant blockbuster, raking in phenomenal record-breaking receipts week after week for months on end and grabbing 11 Oscars. Its theme song by Celine Dion, "My Heart Will Go On," instantly became a favorite funeral hymn. The film so captured the imagination of viewers on every continent that many returned to see it again and again, upwards of 10 times, swamping theaters and forcing them to offer more showings. Austere Asian governments became concerned over the amount of money their financially strapped people were wasting at the box office. A $600 million full-size replica was announced to be ready for the ninetieth anniversary of the ship's sinking. According to organizers, tickets for the April

2002 voyage would cost $10,000 to $100,000. This *Titanic* will not sink, they claim.

Because of the movie, for a second time in less than a year a global village was awash in disaster, gripped with the unthinkable! Are we next?

Beauty, youthfulness, money, sex, love, power, influence, fame, class status—you can have it all and still die. Unexpectedly. Tragically. Then what? If the most luminous woman in the world can die, what about us? If the ship even God couldn't sink still went under on its luxurious maiden voyage, aborting a sweet romance and extinguishing thousands of lives, who can assure the unthinkable won't happen again—to us? The haunting unspoken reality about Princess Diana's life and death is that somewhere amid all her youthfulness, generosity, beauty, wealth, influence, and the grip of the imagination of millions, God, moral virtue, and eternal hope were strangely absent. Cameron's *Titanic* also provides no hope, only a perilous moral journey downward toward death and inconceivable heartache. The scene of a single lifeboat returning to search the midnight waters for survivors is poignant—chilling darkness, eerie death, frightening silence, and the nagging question "Why?"

"'Meaningless! Meaningless!' says the Teacher. 'Utterly meaningless! Everything is meaningless'" (Eccl. 1:2, NIV). Could Solomon have more accurately described the existential angst of our postmodern generation haunted by countless unthinkables?[4] We are fragile candles in the wind. Are we next? "'Meaningless! Meaningless! Utterly meaningless! . . . Everything is meaningless.'" Solomon hits the nail straight on. Written nearly 3,000 years ago, Ecclesiastes speaks with compelling relevance. Its pithy and horribly honest sayings intuitively strike an answering cord in hurting, hopeless hearts—"Been there. Suffered that."

Ecclesiastes is Solomon's journal of his own desperate, torturous journey for meaning. Of his almost-too-late finding that life is meant to be a lifelong love affair with the living God who dwells *above the sun*. Because of its arresting candor and surprising conclusions,

Ecclesiastes is the best news around for our baffled and frightened postmodern world. It's a book for men and women who want to live again—now! The ancient writing speaks to the working person's boredom as he or she struggles with the routine of joylessly eating, drinking, and earning a paycheck. The book appeals to thinking people haunted with questions of identity, meaning, purpose, value, enjoyment, and destiny. And it has much to say to a restless, ambivalent generation haunted by the unthinkable.

Surprisingly, in spite of its assertion that "everything is meaningless" (Eccl. 1:2; 12:8, NIV), the mood of Ecclesiastes is actually one of delight and hope. Ecclesiastes advocates joy and rejoicing because life is a gift from God. But the meaning of life is surprising. The prospect of living and enjoying all of life's goods is inextricably linked with the fullness of a life spent in fellowship with a loving personal God. Coming to terms with reality brings us face-to-face with God!

My prayer is that this living God, who delights in restoring the joy of this life and the joy of eternal life to empty, restless men and women haunted by the unthinkable, will use Ecclesiastes and this new book to inspire a lifelong love affair with Himself.

One final word before you open the text of Scripture and the expositions found in the pages that follow. Ecclesiastes has been a book clearly on the margins of the biblical canon and of Christian thinking in general. As Seow writes in his newest addition to the *Anchor Bible* series: "There is perhaps no book in the Bible that is the subject of more controversies than Ecclesiastes. From the start, its place in the canon was called into question largely because it was perceived to be internally inconsistent and partly because it appears to be unorthodox. Down at least to the fifth century of the common era, there were voices of doubt regarding the canonicity of the book. Even in modern times there have been some who have wondered about its authority."[5]

Some ideas in Ecclesiastes don't seem easily to fit in with conventional Christian sentiments or ways of expressing things. It is a book filled with irony, paradoxes, and apparent contradictions. On the surface Ecclesiastes comes across as moralistic, secular, cynical, and fatalistic. It's an enigmatic and elusive book.

Affirming that what Solomon wrote is inspired, I refuse to accept what I have found many scholars saying about Ecclesiastes: that the book is filled with heresies, half-truths, and cynicism.[6] That it reflects a confused man who barely gets a grip on life in the final chapter. Rather, I accept the traditional view, as supported by Ellen White, that Solomon was writing at a time in his life when he finally did have his act together.[7] In fact, God inspired him to share his spiritual journey and to show where the real issues of life lay.[8] I find Ecclesiastes highly candid but solid and trustworthy in its message. There is no getting around what Solomon writes here. The challenge is in understanding what in fact he is saying, and why he puts it the way he does. Could it be that the meaning of the text resides precisely *in* the irony, the paradox, the contradiction?[9] I believe so. Ecclesiastes requires gray matter (demanding thought) and Holy Spirit prompting (spiritual discernment). It will exercise both your mind and soul.

Ecclesiastes was written with an eye to a wider circle of readers than just the Hebrews. As with other wisdom literature, it has a down-to-earth cosmopolitan feel to it. We find a definite missionary flavor to the book as it attempts to use a sort of what we now call "cultural apologetics" to summon people anywhere and everywhere to straighten out their thinking, action, and values, and to prepare for their eternal destiny.[10] Meeting people where they are, Solomon raises both a voice of warning that can save others from the bitter experiences through which he himself has passed, and a voice of hope that can inspire restless hearts with the promise that God Himself can satisfy their soul.

---

[1] "Tribute to Princess Diana," *Time,* Sept. 15, 1997, pp. 30-75; "Farewell to Diana," *Newsweek,* Sept. 8, 1997, pp. 24-69; "Princess Diana 1961-1997—Special Report," *Newsweek,* Sept. 8, 1997, pp. 26-48; *Time,* Dec. 22, 1997, p. 41; Roger Rosenblatt, "The Year Emotions Ruled," *Time,* Dec. 22, 1997, pp. 64-68.

[2] Richard Lacayo, "Images," *Time,* Dec. 22, 1997, p. 41.

[3] "Rough Waters," *Newsweek*, Dec. 15, 1997, pp. 64-68.

[4] I assume a Solomonic authorship of Ecclesiastes. In Ecclesiastes 1:12 the writer states, "I Qohelet [the Preacher, or Teacher] have been king over Israel in Jerusalem," and verse 1 prefaces the book with the claim: "The words of Qohelet, son of David, king in Jerusalem." Because Solomon was the only immediate son of David who was king over Israel, reigning in Jerusalem, there can be little doubt that he is the one so specified. In supporting the traditional view of Solomonic authorship of Ecclesiastes, Old Testament scholar Walter Kaiser writes, "The predominant ideas found in Ecclesiastes, namely, wisdom and the fear of God, and their application to secular and sacred life likewise fit the character of Solomon as set forth in 1 Kings 3 and the book of Proverbs" (Walter Kaiser, *Ecclesiastes: Total Life* [Chicago: Moody Press, 1979], p. 29). Furthermore, Solomon is said to have a patron and author of wisdom materials (1 Kings 4:32-34; Prov. 1:1; 10:1; 25:1).

[5] See C. L. Seow, *Ecclesiastes* (New York: Doubleday, 1997), p. ix.

[6] See Roy B. Zuck, "A Theology of the Wisdom Books and the Song of Songs," in *A Biblical Theology of the Old Testament*, Roy B. Zuck, ed. (Chicago: Moody Press, 1991), pp. 243-246; Kaiser, p. 15.

[7] Kaiser, pp. 29-31; Ellen G. White, *Prophets and Kings* (Mountain View, Calif.: Pacific Press Pub. Assn., 1970), pp. 77-80.

[8] White, pp. 77-80.

[9] Jacques Ellul, *Reason for Being* (Grand Rapids: William B. Eerdmans Pub. Co., 1990), pp. 40, 41.

[10] Walter C. Kaiser, Jr., p. 32.

1

BEEN THERE. DONE THAT. NOW WHAT?[1]

The words of the Preacher, the Son of David, king in Jerusalem.
"Vanity of vanities," says the Preacher,
"Vanity of vanities! All is vanity."
>   *—Ecclesiastes 1:1, 2*

"Vanities of vanities," says the Preacher, "all is vanity!"
In addition to being a wise man,
>   *the Preacher also taught the people knowledge;*
>   *and he pondered, searched out and arranged many proverbs.*
The Preacher sought to find delightful words
>   *and to write words of truth correctly.*
The words of wise men are like goads,
>   *and masters of these collections are like*
>   *well-driven nails;*
>   *they are given by one Shepherd.*
>   *—Ecclesiastes 12:8-11*

One of the T-shirts my oldest son wears has the silhouette of a basketball player leaping high to slam-dunk a shot, his arms outstretched and body extended as if he's floating in midair. Above the figure are just two words: "He's Back."

Serious basketball fans will remember that autumn day in 1993 when Chicago Bulls superstar Michael Jordan faced a crowded press conference and told them he was retiring. He had suffered no injury, faced no indictments or shocking personal revelations, was involved in no contract disputes. Instead, he was unarguably the game's finest player and was just 30 years old. At the pinnacle of his career—after winning an unprecedented third world championship and seven consecutive NBA scoring titles—he retired.

Jordan told the stunned crowd of media representatives that basketball no longer offered any more challenges to motivate him. "I just feel that I don't have anything else to prove. . . . The desire just isn't there." He had "reached the pinnacle," he said, and had no place to go but down. Having accomplished everything basketball could ask of him, he simply felt it was time to move on. As it was, he was leaving with more money than he could spend in a single lifetime, and was doing so at an age when many are only beginning to taste career success.

Why would a man with everything *under the sun* just walk away?

Jordan, whose father had been murdered earlier in the year, hinted at the answer as he told reporters that one thing about his father's death was that it reinforced "how valuable life is . . . that it can be gone and be taken away from you at any time." [2] The "stuff" of life lost its meaning for Jordan when he considered the fragile transience of it all. Basketball—and the fame, money, and excitement of being better at it than anyone else—no longer was enough. As he looked ahead toward another NBA season, his heart was saying, "Been there. Done that. Now what?" He didn't have an answer, except that he couldn't go on. It was meaningless. He felt bored, restless, empty, and tired of being Michael Jordan. [3]

Been there. Done that. Now what? This sense of detached meaninglessness is not limited to burned-out multimillion-dollar athletes. In 1992 *Forbes* magazine devoted its seventy-fifth anniversary issue to a single topic: "Why we feel so bad when we have it so good." [4] Noting that Americans live better than any other people in the world, *Forbes* invited 11 prominent observers of modern culture to speculate as to why we are so "depressed." Their answers yielded a fairly common thread—an alarming loss of values, absolutes, and meaning in contemporary life.[5] As Saul Bellow asks: "Can it be we are tired of whatever it is that we in fact are?"[6] Peggy Noonan, former CBS newswriter for Dan Rather and speechwriter for both Ronald Reagan and George Bush, asserts that "we are the first generations of man that expected to find happiness here on earth, and our search for it has caused such unhappiness."[7] Philosopher Peter Kreeft suggests that we're a society that has "turned the world into a giant fun-and-games factory, a rich kid's playroom."[8] A society that has the least reason to be bored. Yet we're the most bored, the most restless, the most disillusioned.

Years ago, Israel's King Solomon, a man with more power, more money, more career success, more sex, more fame than Michael Jordan, Bill Gates, or anyone else for that matter—also found himself saying, "Been there. Done that. Now what?" He chronicled his search for the answer in the book we call Ecclesiastes. It's the journal of a desperate journey, a confessional autobiography about chasing the wind, hitting bottom, and hating life. Solomon is saying, "I was chasing the wind" (see Eccl. 1:14); "I hated life" (Eccl. 2:17); "A stillborn child would be better off than me" (see Eccl. 6:3); "Vanity of vanities! All is vanity" (Eccl 1:2).

He begins his journal with emptiness as the bottom line. It's the bottom line on the last page, too (Eccl. 12:8). "Vanity of vanities! All is vanity." Solomon sounds pessimistic. Life is just vapor—what's left when a soap bubble pops. Gum wrappers blowing in the wind. When we add everything up, the sum is zero. Old Solomon looked at all he had done, built, conquered, accomplished. All the women he had loved. All the great ideas floating in his head. And he simply said—"Zilch!" He had everything and still came up empty. He had been living *under the sun,* in a wearisome flatland without meaning and purpose.

What's Life All About?

Ecclesiastes is the book for our generation! I can think of no more accurate picture of our postmodern generation as we rush headlong into the twenty-first century. Ecclesiastes surprisingly mirrors the boredom and restlessness of our times. I believe it reflects, too, the boredom and restlessness of God's last-day people. As an Adventist people—after 150 years of preaching distinctive truths about the soon return of Christ, after generations of careful theology, generations of sensible lifestyle and worship—we find ourselves saying, "Been there. Done that. Now what?" We're bored. Bored as individuals and congregations. God and church leave us bored. What we've been taught, our lifestyle, and worship all bore us, leaving us restless for something more, something different. Unless we come to grips with the message of this book, we will not survive the coming crisis. Each of us needs something deeper than mere theology or eschatology.

The restlessness behind our "Been there. Done that. Now what?" underscores our often desperate search for meaning. In every man and woman lurks a gnawing desire to know what life is all about. We seek something beyond mere activity, intellectual prowess, fame, pleasure, or wealth—even religion and "doing church"! The trouble is that many don't have the foggiest idea as to the meaning of life. That includes, we will find in our study of Ecclesiastes, many who are deeply religious and may profess faith in God and the soon return of Jesus Christ.

Ask a dozen people the meaning of life and you'll get a dozen different answers. *Life* magazine interviewed a number of people about the meaning of life for its 1988 holiday issue.[9] Jose Martinez, a taxi driver, said, "We're here to die, just live and die. I drive a cab. I do some fishing, take my girl out, pay taxes, do a little reading, then get ready to drop dead. You've got to be strong about it. Life is a big fake. . . . You're here, you're gone. You're like the wind. After you're gone, other people will come."[10]

Paleontologist Stephen Jay Gould said: "We are here because one odd group of fishes had a peculiar fin anatomy that could transform into legs for terrestrial creatures; because the earth never froze entirely during the ice age; because a small tenuous species, arising in

Africa a quarter of a million years ago, has managed, so far, to survive by hook and by crook. We may yearn for a 'higher' answer—but none exists. . . . We cannot read the meaning of life passively in the facts of nature. We must construct these answers ourselves—from our own wisdom and ethical sense. There is no other way." [11]

Mother and writer Jamaica Kincaid replied: "If I had been asked why we are here four years ago, just when my daughter was born and I would stand over her as she lay in her little bassinet asleep and just weep uncontrollably because I was beyond happiness or sorrow or any other feeling I had ever known, I would have said that this small child—my child—and all others just like her, was the reason we are here. Just the other day, though, over her objections, I turned off the *Sleeping Beauty* video so that her father and I could watch the evening news. Half to herself, half to the empty space in front of her, not directly at us at all, and in a plaintive voice, she said, 'Now I'm all alone with my boring parents.' If anyone should absolutely, definitely, truthfully find out why we are here, please do not tell me. If I were to really, really know, I feel certain that I should then ask, 'Please, may I now leave?'" [12]

Humorist Garrison Keillor summed up the meaning of life this way: "To know and serve God, of course, is why we're here, a clear truth that, like the nose on your face, is near at hand and easily discernable but can make you dizzy if you try to focus on it hard." [13]

He Was Searching Too

Solomon, too, searched for the meaning of life. "I set my mind to seek and explore by wisdom concerning all that has been done under heaven. It is a grievous task which God has given to the sons of men to be afflicted with" (Eccl. 1:13). The Israelite leader knew by experience that the quest for meaning can be an extremely lonely, disillusioning, and wearying task. And yet he pursued it with a passion. Why? Two passages give the clue:

"Now Solomon loved the Lord, walking in the statutes of his father David, except he sacrificed and burned incense on the high places" (1 Kings 3:3).

"Now King Solomon loved many foreign women. . . . His wives turned his heart away after other gods; and his heart was not wholly devoted to the Lord his God. . . . And Solomon did what was evil in the sight of the Lord, and did not follow the Lord fully" (1 Kings 11:1-6).

That little word "except" is crucial! The phrases "not wholly devoted" and "did not follow fully" are significant! They speak of exceptions, divided loyalties, selective obedience, compromises, and rationalization. Solomon justified his disobedience and selective loyalty by saying that he loved God in spite of it. It is much like some in our day, who "attempt to give life meaning through a general, nebulous, non-challenging belief in God—a God who makes no requirements on the way we live."[14]

A Danish philosopher tells the story of a spider that dropped a single strand down from the top rafter of an old barn and began to weave its web. Days, weeks, and months went by, and the web grew. It regularly provided the spider food as its elaborate maze trapped flies, mosquitoes, and other small insects. The spider built its web larger and larger until it became the envy of all the other spiders. One day as the spider traveled across its beautifully woven web, it noticed a single strand going up into the darkness of the rafters. *I wonder why this is here?* it thought. *It doesn't serve to catch me any dinner.* And saying that, the spider climbed as high as he could and severed the single strand. The entire web slowly began to tumble to the floor of the barn, taking the spider with it.

That's what happened to Solomon. As Ed Young writes, "somewhere along the way . . . Solomon clipped the strand that united him with God *above the sun* and decided to find meaning and satisfaction in a life lived strictly *under the sun.* In other words, he chose a life lived on his own terms, in a natural dimension with no reference to the divine."[15] That little phrase "under the sun" appears 29 times in the book of Ecclesiastes. It describes Solomon's perspective perfectly: one of life viewed from the flatlands. Such life simply has no meaning without God.

Solomon's downward spiral began with simple rationalizations. The result was angst, restlessness, and emptiness. As he says, the search for meaning can be wearisome when you've cut the string. "It is a grievous task which God has given to the sons of men to be afflicted with" (Eccl. 1:13). It's one endless mad whirl!

Newsweek's final issue for 1995 caricatured the previous year in witty cartoons. One of them shows a jumbo jet flying high above cloud level. Off to the left is Michael Jordan, basketball in hand, gliding up through the clouds in his characteristic stretch. Someone inside the plane looks out and says, "Of course, it's gonna take a few more games until he's fully back." [16] Yes, Michael came back—big-time! With a mature passion unseen in his early career. And so did Solomon. He returned with a passion! Solomon soared to the very heart of life's meaning—God. And this time in a deeper, more radical way, with no exceptions, no compromises, no rationalizations, no dividing loyalties. In the end he found that "there is only one thing that never gets boring: God." [17] Listen to how he says it at the close of chapter 5: "For they will scarcely brood over the days of their lives, because God keeps him occupied with the joy of their hearts" (Eccl. 5:20, NRSV).

His wearying, soul-afflicting search for meaning came to an end. He ceased wondering about "who I am" or "where I'm going." Boredom, empty restlessness, and fear of death, tragedy, or the uncertainties of life all vanished. "God keeps him occupied with gladness of heart."

That's Ecclesiastes' message for our postmodern, restless age: to find God and to know God is real life. Augustine puts it this way: "He who has God has everything. He who does not have God has nothing. He who has God and everything has no more than he who has God and nothing." [18]

Only one thing never gets boring: God!

Well-driven Nails

And so we have Solomon's "well-driven nails" (Eccl. 12:11):

Ecclesiastes and all its pithy and horribly honest sayings. The book is Solomon's journal of his desperate, torturous journey for meaning, his almost-too-late finding out that God meant life to be a lifelong love affair with the living God who dwells *above the sun.*

The ancient writing contains no hopeful Gumpisms,[19] no questions and conclusions of a folksy idiot such as Forest Gump, the movie character who captured the imagination of many trying to put it all together on their own because they can no longer trust the experts, or anything, for that matter. "We should never hesitate to listen to a fool about life because life is pretty foolish as far as I can tell. And the great thing about hearing from a birdbrain is that we can all understand what he's saying," declared P. J. O'Rourke.[20] "I don't know if we have a destiny or we're just like a feather just being blown around by the wind. Maybe it's both," Forest Gump tells Jenney, the love of his life, at her graveside.

No! This biblical book has no Gumpisms. Ecclesiastes gives us well-driven nails of honest truth correctly written—"The words of wise men are like goads, and masters of these collections are like *well-driven nails"* (Eccl. 12:11). They are honest truth for our bored and restless age. More than that they are honest truth for a final generation, honest truth for a remnant people struggling for meaning and who want to know what's really important. It hits the nail on the head in terms of all the painful and idiotic things we do in our search for meaning. Ecclesiastes sets a straight nail in the wall for us to hang our thoughts, hang our hearts, our hope, our remnant faith.

I invite you to join me in Solomon's search for meaning. Follow me in his journey until we find why "he's back." And hopefully, like him, we will discover that knowing the living God is more than enough. That He alone can occupy our hearts with gladness.

Do you know God like that? Does He occupy your heart with gladness? Or are you restless, bored, and empty inside? When you get where you are going, where will you be?

God didn't abandon Solomon. Nor will He abandon you. So listen up.

[1] I am indebted for the inspiration of this chapter to Ed Young's book by the same title: *Been There. Done That. Now What? The Meaning of Life May Surprise You* (Nashville: Broadman and Holman Publishers, 1994).

[2] "I'll Fly Away," *Time,* Oct. 18, 1993, pp. 114-116; "The Desire Isn't There," *Sports Illustrated,* Oct. 18, 1993, pp. 28-35.

[3] Ed Young, *Been There. Done That. Now What? The Meaning of Life May Surprise You* (Nashville: Broadman and Holmon Publishers, 1994), pp. 7, 8; "I'll Fly Away," *Time,* p. 115.

[4] *Forbes,* Sept. 14, 1992.

[5] James W. Michaels, "Oh, Our Aching Angst," *Forbes,* Sept. 14, 1992, p. 54.

[6] Saul Bellow, "There Is Simply Too Much to Think About," *Forbes,* Sept. 14, 1992, p. 98.

[7] Peggy Noonan, "You'd Cry Too if It Happened to You," *Forbes,* Sept. 14, 1992, p. 65.

[8] See Peter Kreeft, *Back to Virtue* (San Francisco: St. Ignatius Press, 1992), pp. 156, 157.

[9] "The Meaning of Life," *Life,* December 1988, pp. 76-93.

[10] *Ibid.,* p. 80.

[11] *Ibid.,* p. 84.

[12] *Ibid.,* p. 83.

[13] *Ibid.,* p. 82.

[14] Young, p. 18.

[15] *Ibid.,* pp. 15, 16.

[16] *Newsweek,* Dec. 25, 1995/Jan. 1, 1996, p. 92.

[17] Kreeft, p. 157.

[18] As quoted by Kreeft, p. 157.

[19] Winston Groom, *Gumpisms: The Wit and Wisdom of Forrest Gump* (New York: Pocket Books, 1994).

[20] *Ibid.,* p. vi.

57 CHANNELS
AND NOTHIN'S ON

What advantage does man have in all his work which he does under
the sun?
A generation goes and a generation comes, but the earth
remains forever.
Also, the sun rises and the sun sets; and hastening to its place it rises
there again.
Blowing toward the south, then turning toward the north,
the wind continues swirling along; and on its circular
courses the wind returns.
All the rivers flow into the sea, yet the sea is not full.
To the place where the rivers flow, there they flow again.
All things are wearisome; man is not able to tell it.
The eye is not satisfied with seeing, nor is the ear filled with hearing.
That which has been is that which will be, and that which has been
done is that which will be done.
So, there is nothing new under the sun.
Is there anything of which one might say, "See this, it is new"?
Already it has existed for ages which were before us.
There is no remembrance of earlier things;
and also of the later things which will occur,
there will be for them no remembrance among those who
will come later still.

—*Ecclesiastes 1:3-11*

The "Adventurer" claimed to enable you to experience skiing a mountain trail in your own home. So you get NordicTrack's newest model with interactive video electronics that matches the resistance of your workout to the slope of the trail you watch on your TV. The videotape includes three absolutely breathtaking trails. Getting on it, you see awe-inspiring scenery. And you go . . . nowhere! No matter which trail you choose, no matter how hard you puff and sweat or your legs burn and sides ache, no matter how breathtaking the trail you choose, when you get off, you're in the same place you began. A quick reality check will confirm that you are, in fact, still in your own home.

I've got a NordicTrack. Not the one with the interactive video, but I know what it's like to stand there and expend as much energy as possible for as long as possible while I'm going absolutely nowhere. But I had never cross-country skied in my life until just recently when my family shared Christmas in Vermont with my wife's brother. For the first time I experienced the reality of using all that body energy and coordinated motion to actually go somewhere—up a real hill, down a real snow-laden trail. It was exhilarating—and real!

Solomon knew what it was like to expend a lot of life energy down various supposedly breathtaking trails only to come away with that haunting inner feeling that he'd really gone nowhere. In fact, he had been going nowhere fast as he chased the wind. So he asked himself, "What advantage does a man have in all his work which he does under the sun?" (Eccl. 1:3). Sound familiar? The key word is "advantage," which comes from the original Hebrew word meaning "that which is left over when the transaction is complete." We would say, "When it is all said and done, when you turn the light out at the end of life—what's left? What do you have? What did you accomplish? What purpose has there been to your life and all you've done? What meaning is there beyond the moment? When you get where you are going, where will you be?"

The monotonous drag of everyday life is an undeniable fact of reality. Sometimes it seems like an endless and wearisome cycle of sunrise and sunset. And in between—the same old thing. Too many of us get up in the morning, go to work, come home, and go to bed—and then repeat the cycle day in and day out. Before we know it, life has slipped by. And we ask ourselves, So what? What for? Like Frank Domofio, the barber: "I've been asking why I'm here most of my life. If there's a purpose I don't care anymore. I'm 74; I'm on my way out. Let the young people learn the hard way, like I did. No one ever told me anything."[1]

How many of us see no future in our employment, little hope in our marriages, a lack of challenge in our personal pursuits, and strong feelings of doubt that our lives have any lasting meaning and purpose?

What's New, Man?

To answer our question, Solomon gives us some straight facts about human existence, regardless of how disturbing we may find them. They were things he had learned as he butted his head up against reality. What he has to say are well-driven nails for us to find purpose through.

First, Solomon reminds us of how life here *under the sun* always seems to be moving in cycles but going nowhere. He presents some examples for us to chew on. The passing of generations (Eccl. 1:4). The rhythmic cycles of nature (verses 6, 7). The absence of something new (verses 9, 10). And the disheartening certainty that in time, we along with our generation will be forgotten (verse 11). It's that last one that really gets us—that we won't be remembered.

I had a funeral once for a man whose wife I had buried a decade earlier. All they had were each other. They were not religious people, nor did they have any children. But they loved the raccoons, birds, deer, and squirrels and had installed elaborate feeders to care for their animal friends. The man had spent the last 10 years of his life painfully clinging to the memory of his wife. She was gone for good. They had no hope of being together again. Being remembered was it. So upon his death, his estate was to provide permanently for those an-

28

imals, and the new owners of his property were to keep the couple's memory alive. When you saw a deer or bird or raccoon, you were to think of him and his wife. No wonder Solomon writes in the first part of verse 8: "All things are wearisome: man is not able to tell it." The monotonous rhythm of life can get pretty tiring. "How do you make sense out of it?" he asks. When you're gone, so what? It's ironic that the human beings God created to rule and subdue the earth are the ones who disappear while the earth and its ceaseless cycles remain.

Second, Solomon shares an incredible insight into our human nature—"the eye is not satisfied with seeing, nor is the ear filled with hearing" (verse 8). Here we are, he says, caught in the monotonous drag of life *under the sun,* but God wired us for novelty. We have an itch for change, an appetite for something new. We all crave something bigger, better, prettier, or more pleasurable. No matter what we see or hear, we continue to look for things more pleasing to the eye. Rocker Bruce Springsteen's song "57 Channels (and Nothin' On)" comes close to the idea. We surf the channels of life looking for something that will catch our eye—to be sure we're not missing anything. Why? Because of our insatiable thirst for newness.

Our modern world feeds our insatiable appetite for novelty by coming out with new products, new video games, new movies, new models of everything. The list is endless, whether we really need them or not. Hey, its new, different, better. Break the monotony. Go for it! We see it in every area of life: church, amusement, fashion, food.

One afternoon I was walking toward the parking lot by the School of Business and the Theological Seminary on the campus of Andrews University when I heard a loud throbbing, pounding noise that just wouldn't quit. And it grew louder with every step. Glancing toward the parking lot, I saw a sleek black sports car with deep black Mafia-style windows. Someone had its stereo on full blast. The music boomed so loudly that the whole car seemed as if it were rocking back and forth. After purposely walking by it on my way to my own car, I couldn't believe my eyes. Inside some guy sat reading a book! When we like something, we can't get enough of it.

Something in us keeps us always looking and listening, Solomon says. We're searching. Our appetite for change drives our inner restlessness and the reality that the sameness of life lived here *under the sun* will never satisfy. In spite of our hunger for something new, however, "there is nothing new under the sun. Is there anything of which one might say, 'See this, it is new'? Already it has existed for ages" (verses 9, 10).

Is it really true that there's nothing new *under the sun?* Do you believe nothing new exists in our world today? What about notebook computers? virtual reality? laser surgery? or space stations? What's Solomon talking about? His point, I believe, is that our human race does not progress. We may have advances in science and technology, but we *are* nothing new. Events change, the conditions of life and the standards of living alter, but people stay the same. We remain trapped in our mortality. Yes, an enormous difference exists in the way Genghis Khan killed (with a saber) and our way (nuclear bombs), but our human behavior pattern is the same. Murder, envy, domination, lust—they do not change. The seven deadly sins still exist.[2] Citizens of constantly altering progress, we find it hard to believe or accept that we're faced with the same monotonous drag of life that Solomon faced 3,000 years ago. After all is said and done, our human condition continues, our restless hunger for something new remains.

Worldview Matters

During a *Monitor Radio News* interview, someone asked former astronaut Charles Conrad about his historic space walk. What was it like to crawl outside of his Apollo spacecraft and walk in space? Conrad told of seeing our little planet from outer space, then spoke of the difference of perspective between looking at our earth through the Apollo spacecraft window and getting out there on the walk. You see more when you're outside! He described his experience of sensing a whole new reality—the captivating beauty of blue wrapped with cotton-white clouds, the sense of speed, how often the sun rises and sets in one day of orbit, how our planet is absolutely nothing against the expanse of outer space. That's what we need— a different perspective, a glimpse of the larger picture.

I want us to catch the main theme in Solomon's thought—it's the little phrase "under the sun." Appearing 29 times in the book of Ecclesiastes, it describes our common worldview perfectly. We look at life through the spacecraft window, thus seeing only part of reality. For Solomon, that means trying to find the meaning of life outside a God-centered universe. But we desperately need to view life from another angle—from *above the sun*. Solomon puts it this way: "For God is in heaven and you are on earth; therefore let your words be few" (Eccl. 5:2). Hey, there's a larger picture—a view from *above the sun* that reflects God's perspective. And if you let it, that *above the sun* vantage will change even your choice of words.

The heart of this *above the sun* view is that our world is moving toward a specific goal and that the living God takes each of us very seriously. How do we know? One of the *above the sun* themes running through Ecclesiastes is that of the judgment.

"I have seen under the sun that in the place of justice there is wickedness, and in the place of righteousness there is wickedness. I said to myself, 'God will judge both the righteous man and the wicked man,' for a time for every matter and for every deed is there" (Eccl. 3:16, 17).

"Rejoice, young man, during your childhood, and let your heart be pleasant during the days of young manhood. And follow the impulses of your heart and the desires of your eyes. Yet know that God will bring you to judgment for all these things" (Eccl. 11:9).

"The conclusion, when all has been heard, is: fear God and keep His commandments, because this applies to every person. For God will bring every act to judgment, everything which is hidden, whether it is good or evil" (Eccl. 12:13, 14).

The judgment provides a framework of meaning for our everyday lives. The living God takes us seriously—our words, our thoughts, our actions, even the hidden things. We're not talking about the documented life in which Big Brother keeps you in check or runs out to get you if you mess up (Bill Gates tells about a future that will have cameras on street corners, and Dan Rather reports about gunshot detecting devices on street corners that will give their exact locations on monitors). It's more profound than that.

Our modern world asks what meaning there is beyond the moment. The judgment affirms that our world is headed toward a goal. That we live in a moral universe in which we are significant and accountable. It tells us that the seemingly humdrum routine of life builds character. Even in the midst of everyday life we can know, love, obey, and honor God. Life is no meaningless endless flow—a "row, row, row, your boat, gently down the stream; merrily, merrily, merrily, merrily, life is but a dream" kind of thing. Every moment has value and dignity for the purpose of knowing and honoring the living God of heaven.

While our passage reminds us that humanity has not really changed through the passing generations, the judgment affirms that we as individuals can. We can have a sense of purpose and destiny. Catching that larger picture, we can through God's grace choose to live in harmony with that viewpoint.

That's why the first angel of Revelation 14 shouts its appeal to our final generation: "Fear God and give glory to Him, for the hour of His judgment has come" (Rev. 14:7, NKJV). It's a truth that none of us living in this restless generation of ours dare take lightly. But it's not enough just to know intellectually that God is in heaven and we are on earth, and that the long view measures the purpose of life against the coming judgment. We must know God Himself, must come to the place where to have Him is to have everything. Here's how the apostle Paul puts it:

"If then you have been raised up with Christ, keep seeking the things above, where Christ is, seated at the right hand of God. Set your mind on the things above, not on the things that are on earth. For you have died and your life is hidden with Christ in God. When

Christ, who is our life, is revealed, then you also will be revealed with Him in glory" (Col. 3:1-4, NRSV).

The problem is that we're talking now about things we can't see or hear. If we have eyes and ears that are never satisfied with the world we can perceive, how in the world can we ever get excited about something we can't really see or hear?

Setting our mind on things above is the key! An American Indian and his friend walked together in downtown Manhattan. As they pushed through the seething humanity, the din and noise of the big city, the Indian caught the sound of a cricket. When he mentioned to his friend that he had heard a cricket, his friend laughed. "How can you hear a cricket in this kind of noise, with all the cars and horns and boom boxes?"

Stooping down, the Indian pushed some trash away from the curb and revealed the chirping cricket. "It all depends on what you're listening for and where your interests lie," the Indian said. "Most people here would miss the cricket, but watch this." Reaching into his pocket, the Indian pulled out a handful of change and hurled it down the sidewalk. Suddenly a crowd of otherwise absorbed people began searching for the coins they had heard drop. Their ears were tuned to the sound of money, but not crickets. It all depends on what we're listening for, looking for.

"Now faith is the assurance of things hoped for, the conviction of things not seen. . . . And without faith it is impossible to please Him, for he who comes to God must believe that He is, and that He is a rewarder of those who seek Him" (Heb. 11:1-6). When we lift our gaze *above the sun* toward the living God of heaven, we will find Him!

---

[1] "The Meaning of Life," *Life,* December 1988.

[2] J. Ellul, *Reason for Being,* p. 65.

WE'LL BURN OUR SKIS FOR UHLER

I said to myself, "Come now, I will test you with pleasure.
So enjoy yourself." And behold, it too was futility.
I said of laughter, "It is madness," and of pleasure, "What does
it accomplish?"
I explored with my mind how to stimulate my body with wine
while my mind was guiding me wisely, and how to take hold
of folly, until I could see what good there is for the sons of
men to do under heaven the few years of their lives.
I enlarged my works: I built houses for myself, I planted vineyards
for myself;
I made gardens and parks for myself, and I planted in them all
kinds of fruit trees;
I made ponds of water for myself from which to irrigate a forest
of growing trees.
I bought male and female slaves, and I had homeborn slaves.
Also I possessed flocks and herds larger than all who preceded me
in Jerusalem.
Also, I collected for myself silver and gold, and the treasure of kings
and provinces.
I provided for myself male and female singers and the pleasures of
men—many concubines.
Then I became great and increased more than all who preceded me
in Jerusalem.

My wisdom also stood by me.
And all that my eyes desired I did not refuse them.
I did not withhold my heart from any pleasure,
> *for my heart was pleased because of all my labor and this*
> *was my reward for all my labor.*
Thus I considered all my activities which my hands had done and
> *the labor which I had exerted,*
> *and behold all was vanity and striving after wind*
> *and there was no profit under the sun.*
>
> —*Ecclesiastes 2:1-11*

He was writing a graduate essay exam that should have taken four hours, but he finished it in just 15 minutes. The professor of his psychology class had posed the question: "What is life?" "I just sat around," Scott Salinski said, "kinda looked around for a little bit, and I rephrased it to say, 'Life is everything.' I turned it in and got an A on it. You think about it . . . life is everything. Everything we know is life. And as far as [I'm concerned] . . . it's living for a good time." A good time for Scott is floating at 30 miles an hour downhill on two feet of powder with a big grin on his face. The six-foot-four blond-haired former Aspen ski instructor lives for the adrenaline rush on the Colorado slopes. When the snow really dumps, family, work, and ambition drop way down on his list. In fact, he has no ambition at all—except to ski.

Scott says he believes in Uhler. "Do you know about Uhler?" he asks with a big grin. "Uhler to most of the skiers is the ski god. And in Breckenridge every spring they offer back to Uhler a big bonfire of skis they're not gonna ski with. It's another excuse for a big party," he observes with a laugh. "But anything for a party . . . sure, Uhler! Uhler Day. Great! He gives us skis, he gives us snow, so, yeah, we'll burn our skis for Uhler."[1]

Living for a good time sums up our modern, pleasure-driven generation. We can state the bottom line in just six words: "If it feels good, do it." The words may not appear in bold bronze letters on every wall, but they permeate our modern culture. Sometimes people openly state them. Most of the time they are subliminal—placed there by those who author our books, compose our music, design our clothing, publish our magazines, or direct our films. Whether it's MTV, Jay Leno, bungee jumping, Disney World, Häagen-Dazs double chocolate ice cream, or the casino boat advertisement that says "The world was made in six days but it takes seven to forget it," it's the same: "If it feels good, do it."

The restlessness we learned about in our last chapter really goes bonkers when it comes to finding pleasure. Just think of all the sensory possibilities our bodies have. Or the many ways we can stimulate the endorphins in our brain. Pleasure is the simplest, easiest, most obvious, most promising answer to the search for happiness and meaning. That's because pleasure appears so empirical. It's rock-solid evidence that life *is* good. And right now!

So that's where Solomon started his search for meaning. He decided to scratch some itches that had been there all his life, deep down in the pleasure zone. With intense commitment and tremendous financial resources, he set out to experience self-gratification to the utmost. "I said to myself, 'Come now, I will make a test of pleasure; enjoy yourself'" (Eccl. 2:1, RSV). "All right! I'm going to really check it out," he announced. And he didn't hold back. Take a look at verse 10: "Whatever my eyes desired I did not keep from them; I kept my heart from no pleasure" (RSV). Solomon lived like a kid in a candy store, wanting one of everything he saw. And because he had the means to get it, there was nothing he didn't try. He didn't withhold any pleasure from his heart, because he considered it as his right. "Hey, man, I got it coming to me!" he says in verse 10. "I worked for it."

It was a total plunge into hedonism, the bungee jump of a lifetime. Solomon got to do what many only dream about. He had the proverbial wine, women, and song. The Israelite king brought in the stand-up comedians of his day and became a connoisseur of fine wine and delectable foods. And 1,000 women—unbelievable! They were available to him any time of the day or night, any number at a time, to fulfill whatever sensual fantasy he had. "The delights of the heart of man," he calls it all in verse 8 (NIV).

Wow! we say to ourselves. It doesn't sound like our modern "wild 'n' crazy fun 'n' games" world is so modern after all, does it? In fact, every generation finds itself confronted with the lure of a "this moment, let's have it now" quest for pleasure. Ellen White tells us that the lure for pleasure will be the special temptation for God's last-day people who await the return of Jesus. Speaking of Israel's apostasy at the Jordan River, she writes: "All along through the ages there are strewn wrecks of character that have been stranded upon the rocks of sensual indulgence. As we approach the close of time, as the people of God stand upon the borders of the heavenly Canaan, Satan will, as of old, redouble his efforts to prevent them from entering the goodly land."[2]

I Said to Myself . . .

The interesting thing to me is how Solomon tried to be a "controlled" party animal. He says: "I searched with my mind how to cheer my body with wine—my mind still guiding me with wisdom" (Eccl. 2:3, RSV). "Hey, I could handle my drink," he says. That's important, you know. No one really ever wants to go over the edge. They just want to push it—to get as much adrenaline, as many endorphins as possible. But pushing the edges of the envelope called pleasure can be lethal. A lifestyle devoted to pleasure is empty at best, deadly at worst.[3] Solomon found it ended in nothing but an emotional pileup. All that pleasure had no meaning. "Thus I considered all my activities which my hands had done and the labor which I had exerted, and behold all was vanity and striving after the wind and there was no profit under the sun" (verse 11). Why?

First, Solomon learned the reality of the law of diminishing returns. It declares that after time the same effort produces less satisfaction, so we put more into our passion—whatever it may be—just to enjoy it as much as we did yesterday. Psychologists tell us that we have a "pleasure center" in our brain, a point in the septal region that when stimulated enables us to experience pleasure. Electrodes implanted in this area will produce enjoyment when activated. An animal, for example, can have electrodes hooked up to its brain and be taught to press a bar to receive stimulation in this part of the brain. And the animals learn quickly to use that bar! Rats have been known to press such a bar of their own accord as many as 5,000 times an hour. That's 83 times a minute, 1.3 times a second. It can get pretty boring after a while, except that you don't realize it at the time. The drive for pleasure is so strong that hungry rats would rather stimulate their pleasure centers than eat. In one experiment a rat pressed the bar more than 2,000 times an hour for 24 consecutive hours. Finally it collapsed of hunger and thirst.

Obviously, humans aren't rats, but pleasure seeking is a powerful human drive that can significantly control our behavior. More important, research has shown that the pleasure center of our brain can be overstimulated to the point that it becomes numb and unresponsive.[4] After the surge we crash, each time lower and harder, until life no longer has any real joy. Here's how comedian and television star Jerry Seinfeld puts it: "Everybody's looking for good sex, good food, and a good laugh. They're little islands of relief in what's often a painful existence."[5]

The reality is that once you've left that hilarious comedy show, eaten that $5 piece of chocolate mousse pie, felt the passion of sexual release—life is still life! You're still behind on your credit cards, your boss still treats you unfairly, your kids are still in trouble at school, and you're still not smart enough to make the grade or fast enough to belong to the team. Such so-called "little islands of relief" are phantoms that leave us raw and empty. To put it bluntly, sensual pleasure makes promises that lack staying power.[6] You can see it in people's faces.

Second, Solomon discovered that he was out there on his own, just listening to himself. Who advised Solomon to pursue a pleasure-seeking lifestyle? No one. He simply followed his own inner urges. "I said to myself," he writes, " 'Come now, I will test you with pleasure. So enjoy yourself' " (Eccl. 2:1). I find it interesting that Solomon didn't tap a seasoned counselor on the shoulder and ask for advice. "Hey, you've been over the road. Tell me what this will mean. Where are the potholes?" Nor did he reflect on his father's life or ask God for guidance. He did what most of us do when it comes to the quest for happiness through pleasure—we decide for ourselves! Sometimes defiantly. Sometimes headlong. It's a "nobody's going to tell me what to do" kind of thinking. The rush to gratify our desires is simply an outgrowth of who we are in our hearts. Our decision to listen to ourselves, to seize the moment, comes from within. Proverbs 3:5, 6 exhorts us to "trust in the Lord with all your heart, and do not lean on your own understanding. In all your ways acknowledge Him, and He will make your paths straight." Instead, Solomon lived by the slogan made popular by Frank Sinatra: "I did it my way."

But what happens when we listen only to ourselves? What results when you're out there on your own, *under the sun,* without God? Joy Davidman puts it candidly: "Living for his own pleasure is the least pleasurable thing a man can do; if his neighbors don't kill him in disgust, he will die slowly of boredom and lovelessness."[7]

We become powerless as well—morally and spiritually powerless. Powerless to find meaningful spiritual things, whether they be worship, prayer, Scripture, or God! We become unable to look beyond ourselves and our own gratification and ignore our spouse, children, the needs of other people, and God's work. Lacking a clear view of Jesus and a sense of our need of Him, we can no longer perceive truth, love it, and honor God in the final generation.

White Clothes, Oiled Heads

Enough with the negative stuff! Ecclesiastes presents a balanced view of pleasure, a better way. In fact, I find it fascinating to see how the surprising advice "Enjoy!" punctuates the whole book. Listen to a couple of lines:

"What I have seen is this: that it is good and proper for a man to eat and drink and enjoy himself" (Eccl. 5:18, NEB).

"So I commended pleasure, for there is nothing good for a man under the sun except to eat and to drink and to be merry, and this will stand by him in his toils throughout the days of his life which God has given him under the sun" (Eccl. 8:15).

"Go to it then, eat your food and enjoy it, and drink your wine with a cheerful heart; . . . Always be dressed in white and never fail to anoint your head. Enjoy life with a woman you love all the days of your allotted span here under the sun" (Eccl. 9:7-9, NEB).

"Rejoice, young man, during your childhood, and let your heart be pleasant during the days of young manhood. And follow the impulses of your heart and the desires of your eyes" (Eccl. 11:9).

Solomon is no killjoy whose mission is to keep anyone from having a good time. God has given us the capacity for pleasure. And He says, "Go for it!" But do so in a different way than our "if it feels good, do it" world. No philosophy of life can safely be built on pleasure and the quest for happiness through pleasure, but the biblical philosophy of life includes innocent human pleasure and affirms happiness.

Let's get an *above the sun* view. Here are five nails Solomon drives into the wall for us to hang our pleasure on:

First, eat, drink, enjoy, and be happy when pleasure comes. When days of happiness occur, don't torment yourself with thoughts of all that could happen to wreck your joy, or all the reasons such happiness may be incomplete. Don't be discouraged that your pleasure is only for the moment. When you are happy, don't be on guard—indulge in simple pleasure. Don't permit gloomy thoughts on a holiday! It is to be a time of happiness.[8]

Second, learn to find your happiness in the innocent things of life. Be happy with the simple means of human happiness: food, love, a good day's work, the things you create and do.[9]

Third, understand that real happiness from human pleasure is a gift from God. Solomon asks, "Apart from him [God] who can eat or who can have enjoyment?" (Eccl. 2:24, 25, RSV). The answer is obvious. No one! We must understand the relationship between happiness and God's gift. God empowers us to find happiness. Inner joy and happiness is His gift to us. "Furthermore, as for every man to whom God has given riches and wealth, He has also empowered him to eat from them and to . . . rejoice; . . . this is the gift of God" (Eccl. 5:19). Happiness is a divine gift and we can rejoice that He gives us it.[10]

Fourth, we need to learn to express our happiness in life's simple pleasures. "Go to it then, eat your food and enjoy it, and drink your wine with a cheerful heart. . . . Always be dressed in white and never fail to anoint your head" (Eccl. 9:7, 8, NEB). Allow your pleasure to show. Don't forget the special holiday clothes or the sweet perfume. Look like you're having a good time. Give outward indication that you're enjoying God's good blessings. Let others see it shining in your life. The final generation will not be a generation of "Sadventists," rather they will have joy in the Lord and His goodness.

Pleasures Forever

Fifth, remember that your ultimate happiness will only ever come from knowing God Himself. That's the incredible promise of Ecclesiastes: that in some marvelous unexplainable way God can be known—and loved. He can keep our hearts so occupied with gladness that we're no longer worried about life and how long we'll be here. "He seldom reflects on the days of his life, because God keeps him occupied with gladness of heart" (Eccl. 5:20, NIV). Here's our invitation to find our ultimate happiness, our ultimate pleasure in God. Then all our other lesser pleasures will find their true place and value in our lives. This is what God's remnant people need to experience and show to a lost world.

Is it really possible? Yes! God promises it. He yearns for us to experience it with Him. As Revelation 3:20 tells us, "Behold, I stand at the door and knock; if anyone hears My voice and opens the door, I will come in to him, and will dine with him, and he with Me." God promises not temporary gratification, but lasting joy. He assures us of a place with Himself, in whose presence is fullness of joy, and in whose right hand are *pleasures forever.*

So if you're searching for happiness, don't listen to your own heart or party harder. Instead, pursue God!

[1] Phillip L. Berman, *The Search for Meaning: Americans Talk About What They Believe and Why* (New York: Ballantine Books, 1990), pp. 186-189.

[2] Ellen G. white, *Patriarchs and Prophets* (Mountain View, Calif.: Pacific Press Pub. Assn., 1890), p. 457.

[3] E. Young, *The Meaning of Life,* p. 37.

[4] Archibald D. Hart, *Fifteen Principles for Achieving Happiness* (Dallas: Word Publishing, 1988), pp. 116, 117.

[5] Mark Morrison, "Fall Preview—The *US* Interview: Jerry Seinfeld," *US,* September 1992, p. 37.

[6] Charles Swindoll, *Living on the Ragged Edge Bible Study Guide* (Waco, Tex.: Word Books, 1985), p. 16.

[7] Joy Davidman, *Smoke on the Mountain: An Interpretation of the Ten Commandments* (Philadelphia: Westminster Press, 1985), p. 24.

[8] J. Ellul, *Reason for Being,* p. 109.

[9] *Ibid.*

[10] *Ibid.,* pp. 106-111.

LIFE BETWEEN BOOKENDS— NO TIME-OUTS

There is an appointed time for everything.
And there is a time for every event under heaven—
A time to give birth, and a time to die;
A time to plant, and a time to uproot what is planted.
A time to kill, and a time to heal;
A time to tear down, and a time to build up.
A time to weep, and a time to laugh;
A time to mourn, and a time to dance.
A time to throw stones, and a time to gather stones;
A time to embrace, and a time to shun embracing.
A time to search, and a time to give up as lost;
A time to keep, and a time to throw away.
A time to tear apart, and a time to sew together;
A time to be silent, and a time to speak.
A time to love, and a time to hate;
A time for war, and a time for peace.
What profit is there to the worker from that in which he toils?
I have seen the task which God has given the sons of men
with which to occupy themselves.
He has made everything appropriate in its time.
He has also set eternity in their heart.

—Ecclesiastes 3:1-11

Superbowl XXX (1996) helps us get a handle on the meaning of this passage. While the Dallas Cowboys and the Pittsburgh Steelers were tossing the coin to see who'd receive first, I was making some last-minute calculations about when our two oldest sons might return home from watching the game with some friends who had just gotten a big-screen TV. After all, school was still on the next day, and they had to get to bed at a decent time. "How long does this thing go?" I asked as we bolted out the door, hoping that they'd get there in time to see that first kickoff. For a father who doesn't know very much about a football—except that it's bigger than a Ping-Pong ball and you run it around the field in hopes no one will pulverize you—I knew my question revealed my ignorance. So my 13-year-old just kinda put it in perspective for me. "Dad," he said with an air of confidence, "a football game lasts an hour, but it can take three or more hours to play it."

Oh! I thought to myself. *I never heard it put that way before. I guess it's all those time-outs,* I mused as we squealed out of the garage.

That's when I thought of Ecclesiastes and the idea of life between bookends. Our passage says it so clearly. Birth and death are the bookends of our life *under the sun.* They are divinely appointed, not selected, dates, and so is everything in between. "There is," wrote Solomon, "an appointed time for everything. And there is a time for every event under heaven" (Eccl. 3:1). It all starts with the bookends, i.e., "a time to be born and a time to die" (verse 2, NKJV). Everything "in between" these two boundaries of life takes place while the clock is still ticking. At least that's how Solomon sees it. Between the bookends—between the moment our bottom gets spanked, causing us to draw in that first breath, and the day the coroner writes our certificate of death—we face the full range of life's experiences. Time accommodates every aspect of life—joy, sorrow, love, giving up for lost, rebuilding, and throwing stones. But it does not stop for personal introspection, experimentation, pleasure, or pain. Unlike Superbowl XXX, we have no "time-outs." We can't stop the clock while we think things over and strategize our next play.

44

Like thinkers of every age, Solomon struggled to develop a philosophy that would order and explain the intricacies of life he observed. As he pondered time and the kinds of events that occur in time, he observed that two entirely different perspectives of time overlap in our lives: time as *chronos* and time as *kairos*.[1] *Chronos* time involves duration—mere passing moments that we can measure: a typical day consisting of 86,400 seconds, 1,440 minutes, and 24 hours. Or the number of years one might actually live—67, 83, or just 12. But not all passing moments of time are equally important. We often speak of events as being "timely." *Kairos* identifies a significant moment of time. It's a moment of opportunity involving moral and spiritual value. Such time contains the kind of things Solomon outlines for us as taking place between bookends: "a time to kill, and a time to heal; . . . a time to embrace, and a time to refrain from embracing; . . . a time to keep, and a time to throw away; . . . a time to keep silence, and a time to speak; a time to love, and a time to hate" (Eccl. 3:3-8, NKJV).

Such momentous occasions and opportunities reveal the moral dimension of life lived *under the sun.* Solomon lists 14 pairs of opposites. Twenty-eight times he repeats "time" as he presses home the point of opportunity, decision, and personal accountability. He sensed that while the *chronos* clock is ticking, "timely" events and pivotal opportunities press us for responsible decision and action. Life between bookends is an endless flow of "ordained appointments which open the windows of eternity to us."[2] We have no time-outs! Surely we don't want to be caught laughing when there should be tears in our eyes, or throwing something away that we should have kept, or keeping quiet when we should have spoken up. How we decide, how we respond, in these *kairos* moments expresses moral and spiritual value and determines destiny.

Some *kairos* times are clear and obvious to us. No one then has to tell us "what time it is." Our friend Shirley, who experienced a painful divorce, had her 9-year-old son die in an automobile accident, suffered the ruin of a house fire, and finally lost absolutely everything when Hurricane Andrew destroyed her uninsured home in Homestead, Florida. Each event was a clearly marked *kairos* moment that said, "Shirley, it's time to shun embracing. Time to let go. Time to mourn. To throw away. Stop searching. Rebuild." She tells how after Hurricane Andrew she literally searched and searched for her belongings across block after devastated block but found nothing! The storm had dumped other people's property on her land, but she could find none of hers. It finally came to that *kairos* moment when she became painfully aware that it was time to stop searching.

But sometimes—quite often, in fact—we're not so sure "what time" it really is. We don't really know whether we should keep or discard, love or hate, throw stones or speak up, rebuild or just go on. Sometimes we face real dilemmas. The choices stare us in the face as the clock just keeps ticking away. If we don't know "what time it is," we certainly won't know which course we should pursue. And like Shirley, we're not always sure how we should respond even when we do know what moment lies before us. It may be obvious what time it is, but not so clear how and in what way we should live during it.

Solomon tells us we have a God-given inquisitiveness and capacity to figure things out. We want to understand how our downstairs *under the sun* realm of the ordinary, day-to-day living fits with the upstairs domain of the hereafter. To see how our decisions fit and be satisfied that what we choose in a given moment is the right thing, we want to grasp the larger picture. "What profit is there to the worker from that in which he toils? I have seen the task which God has given the sons of men with which to occupy themselves. He has made everything appropriate in its time. He has also set eternity in their heart, yet so that man will not find out the work which God has done from the beginning even to the end" (Eccl. 3:9-11). All of us want to make sense out of life through the decisions we make. But, Solomon tells us, we're unable to see fully how either the things we experience or our choices fit into a larger meaningful picture. As we well know, the search to understand the present time and then to act appropriately can be both threatening and exasperating.

Everything Appropriate

Once an old woodcutter lived in a tiny village. Although he was poor, everyone envied him, because he owned a beautiful white horse. Even the king coveted his treasure. People offered fabulous prices for the steed, but the old man always refused. The man was poor and the temptation was great, but he never sold the horse. One morning his horse was missing from the stable. All the village came to see him. "You old fool," they scoffed. "We told you that someone would steal your horse. It would have been better for you to have sold it. You could have gotten a handsome price. Now the horse is gone, and misfortune has cursed you."

"Don't speak too quickly," the old man responded. "Say only that the horse is not in the stable. That is all we know; the rest is a case of judgment. If I've been cursed or not, how can you know? How can you judge?"

"Don't make us out to be fools!" the people protested. "We may not be philosophers, but great philosophy is not needed here. The simple fact that your horse is gone is a curse."

"All I know is that the stable is empty," the old man repeated, "and the horse is gone. The rest I don't know. Whether it be a curse or a blessing, I can't say. All we can see is a fragment. Who can say what will come next?"

The people of the village laughed. They thought that the old man was crazy. But after 15 days his prized horse returned. Instead of being stolen, he had run away into the forest. Not only had he returned, but he had brought a dozen wild horses with him. Once again the village people gathered around the old man. "Old man, you were right and we were wrong. What we thought was a curse was a blessing. Please forgive us."

"Once again, you go too far," the old man cautioned. "Say only

47

that the horse is back. State only that a dozen horses returned with him, but don't judge its meaning. How do you know if this is a blessing or not? You see only a fragment. Unless you know the whole story, how can you judge? You read only one page of a book. Can you judge the whole book? Life is so vast, yet you judge all of life with just one page. All you have is a fragment! Don't say this is a blessing. No one knows. I am content with what I know and am not perturbed by what I don't."

"Maybe the old man is right," they said to one another. So they kept silent. But down deep they felt that he was wrong. They believed it had to be a blessing. Twelve horses had returned with one horse. With a little bit of work, the old man could have the animals trained and sell them for much money.

Now, the old man had an only son who began to work with the wild horses. After a few days he fell from one of them and broke both legs. Once again the villagers gathered around the old man and cast their judgments. "You were right," they said. "You proved you were right. The dozen horses were not a blessing. They were a curse. Your only son has broken his legs, and now in your old age you have no one to help you. Now you are poorer than ever."

"You people are obsessed with judging," the old man interrupted. "Don't go so far. Say only that my son broke his legs. Who knows if it is a blessing or a curse? No one knows. We only have a fragment. Life comes in fragments."

It so happened that a few weeks later the country in which they lived found itself at war with a neighboring nation. The king required all the young men of the village to join the army, except the old man's son, who escaped because of his injury. Once again the people came to the old woodcutter, crying and screaming because their sons had been taken off to war. "You were right, old man," they wept. "God knows you were right. This proves it. Your son's accident was a blessing. His legs may be broken, but at least he is with you. Our sons are gone forever."

"It is impossible to talk with you," the old man sighed. "You always draw conclusions. No one knows. Say only this: your sons had to go to war, and mine did not. No one knows if it is a blessing or a curse. No one is wise enough to know. Only God knows."[3]

The old man was right. We have only a fragment of life in our possession at any given time. With just a page between covers it's hard to know what's really happening. How can we know what time it is or how we are to seize the opportunity or show ourselves spiritually and morally responsible? Only God really knows, Solomon declares. And he gives us an incredible nail to hang our *kairos* time on! "He [God] has made everything appropriate in its time" (Eccl. 3:11). Some translations read, "He has made everything beautiful in its time." The Hebrew word *yāreh* means fair, beautiful, excellent. Aesthetically it points to outward appearance. Ethically and spiritually it directs our attention to what is useful, good, appropriate, and right. That's why the NASB reads, "He has made everything appropriate in its time." Ecclesiastes depicts an all-knowing God who is able to make every occasion of life between our bookends an appropriate moment for us spiritually and morally. Each moment is an ordained appointment that opens the windows of eternity for us.

Ecclesiastes 3:11 affirms that life's decision moments have moral and spiritual value. Furthermore, they point to God's ability to lead us through life's moral and spiritual dilemmas. God makes everything appropriate in its time and enables us to sense the time. Helping us to live the time as it should be, God makes it appropriate even though we may not fully understand how it fits.

I believe that when we have faithfully prayed, carefully searched, conscientiously decided, we can move ahead without looking back as to whether we did the right thing or not, because God will make it beautiful!

Life Between Bookends

In January 1967, 20-year-old John W. Lewis's infantry unit received its assignment to the forbidding jungle of Vietnam's Tayninh

Province. On their first maneuver they walked into an ambush. Lewis immediately dropped to his belly, just as instructed in basic training. Bullets and the cries and screams of injured soldiers filled the air. "Stay low," he told himself. For hours the snipers kept them pinned down as they waited for artillery strikes to push the Vietcong back. *This is only the beginning,* Lewis thought to himself. He had just arrived in Vietnam and had a whole year of combat ahead of him— if he survived this attack. While he knew he didn't deserve any special treatment, he found himself praying to live. "God, can You hear me? Are You with me now? Will You stay with me?" he cried.

While his heart pounded and his cheeks were pressed to the ground, Lewis noticed something barely sticking out of the dirt. He reached for a twig and scratched at the spot. The ground was hard, but he kept at it. Finally, he grasped the end of a rusty chain that broke into pieces as he pulled it from the earth. A clump of soil loosened, and he rubbed a tiny object clean. After studying it for a while, he tucked it in the elastic band of his helmet, where it stayed until he was rescued—and until the day he was wounded and flown out of Vietnam several months later. During one of the loneliest moments of his life he had found something lasting and ever present. In a far-off jungle he had unearthed a tiny wooden cross, with the shiny silver figure of One who promised to be always with him and to make everything appropriate in its time.[4]

While Solomon promises that God makes everything appropriate in its time, God doesn't do so in a vacuum. He needs us. We have an important part in the process. Our passage gives the reason God puts eternity in our hearts and yet keeps us from fully understanding "what time it is" or how we should respond accordingly. The end of verse 14 puts it bluntly: "For God has so worked that men should fear Him." Solomon here is talking about an incredible interaction and personal relationship with the living God. It enables us to take each moment of life seriously in the light of His guiding presence and His ability to make all things appropriate both *under the sun* and in light of eternity.

Like Lewis reaching out to God in a critical moment of his

Vietnam tour, we're to seek God for an *above the sun* view. Here's another one of those nails: the invitation to open ourselves to His leading and to determine to do what is good by surrendering our wisdom and acknowledging our limitations. We cannot begin to understand or respond to the decision points of life unless we know Him personally.

This is living life with an *above the sun* view. It takes each moment seriously[5] and reaches out in faith to the living God. We know that through Him life is a set of ordained appointments that open up the windows of eternity to us. It is not fate, not existential choice, not predestination, but a personal relationship with the living God.

Ed Young tells of receiving a Sharper Image catalog that advertised a "Personal Life Clock"—a marble obelisk with digital numbers that flashed the number of hours, minutes, and seconds remaining in one's "statistical lifetime." "All lives are finite," the catalog glibly noted. "In fact, the average life lasts only 683,280 hours, or 2.5 billion seconds. This new Thymuses Personal Life Clock reminds you to live life to the fullest by displaying the . . . most profound number you will ever see."[6] The most profound number you'll ever see? How much time you've got left? No, that's not as important as "what time it is" in your life. The pages between the bookends of our life and our world keep turning slowly. Life offers us no time-outs, just a set of ordained appointments that open for us the issues of eternity.

What time is it in your life? What ordained appointments press you for decisions today? Are you confused with issues confronting you? Do you know which course to choose? Do you have the confidence that God can make everything beautiful, everything appropriate, in its time? Are you in a relationship with Him?

---

[1] Of course, while the concept is biblical, Solomon doesn't use the Greek terms. But his words here along with references to "few years of his life which God has given him" (Eccl. 5:18), "all days of your fleeting life which He has given to you under the sun" (Eccl. 9:9), "few years of his futile life" (Eccl. 6:12), etc., show his sensitivity to both.

[2] Bill and Teresa Syrios, *Ecclesiastes: Chasing After Meaning: 12 Studies for Individuals or Groups* (Downers Grove, Ill.: InterVarsity Press, 1992), p. 21.

[3] Adapted from "The Woodcutter's Wisdom," in Max Lucado, *In the Eye of the Storm* (Dallas: Word Publishing, 1991), pp. 144-147.

[4] John W. Lewis, "Battle Ground," *Guideposts,* February 1996, p. 5.

[5] J. Ellul, *Reason for Being,* p. 237.

[6] E. Young, *The Meaning of Life,* p. 56.

WIRING YOUR BRAIN FOR ETERNITY

And I set my mind to seek and explore by wisdom
concerning all that has been done under heaven.
It is a grievous task which God has given to the sons of men to be
afflicted with.
I have seen all the works which have been done under the sun,
and behold, all is vanity and striving after the wind.
What is crooked cannot be straightened, and what is lacking cannot
be counted.
I said to myself,
"Behold, I have magnified and increased wisdom
more than all who were over Jerusalem before me;
and my mind has observed a wealth of wisdom
and knowledge."
And I set my mind to know wisdom and to know madness and folly;
I realized that this also is striving after wind.
Because in much wisdom there is much grief,
and increasing knowledge results in increasing pain.
—Ecclesiastes 1:13-18

If you take a newborn kitten and sew one of its eyes shut for a few months, what do you think will happen? Will it be able to see out of that eye when you open it again? How about an adult cat?

What happens if you sew one of its eyes shut for a while? Will it be able to use that eye when reopened? That's the kind of stuff you read about in *Newsweek's* February 19, 1996, article entitled "Your Child's Brain." It is a fascinating report on brain development and how our brain's neural circuits wire themselves through early childhood experiences. Circuits in different regions of the brain mature at different times, it says. As a result, different circuits are more sensitive to life's experiences at different ages. Give your children the stimulation they require when they need it, and anything's possible. Deprive them of it, and all bets are off. In other words, with the right input at the right time, your child's brain can develop in almost any direction, gaining abilities in language, music, math, and logic. But if your child misses the window of opportunity, he or she will be playing with a handicap.[1]

By the time we reach adulthood our brain is crisscrossed with more than 100 billion neurons, each reaching out to thousands of others so that, all told, the brain has more than 100 trillion connections. It is those connections—more than the number of galaxies in the known universe—that gives the brain its unrivaled powers. Think of the potential that lies dormant in the brain, needing to be tapped, given the right opportunity. It's enough to motivate all yuppie parents to give their child every opportunity, every advantage. You can influence the way they turn out. If you wire your kids' brains just right, they will be able to do all kinds of stuff.

Solomon was into the brain—his brain. He became enamored with what its possibilities were and what he could do and become with it. Setting his "mind to seek" after anything and everything that would fulfill that potential and give him meaning in life, he became the ultimate professor, the quintessential information man. Gifted by God with wisdom, he pursued it as the highest good, and through education he acquired a wealth of knowledge unequaled in his day. "I have attained greatness, and have gained more wisdom than all who were before me," he says of himself in Ecclesiastes 1:16 (NKJV).

The writer of 1 Kings states that "Solomon's wisdom surpassed the wisdom of all the sons of the east and all the wisdom of Egypt. For he was wiser than all men, than Ethan the Ezrahite, Heman, Calcol and Darda, the sons of Mahol; and his fame was known in all the surrounding nations. He also spoke 3,000 proverbs, and his songs were 1,005. And he spoke of trees, from the cedar that is in Lebanon even to the hyssop that grows on the wall; he spoke of animals and birds and creeping things and fish" (1 Kings 4:30-33).

Solomon was not only book-smart, but creative. A prolific writer and musician, he dabbled in botany and horticulture and was an expert on animals, birds, insects, and fish. People came from all over to hear him. No one could introduce a topic of conversation in which he would not be well-versed. But brains and education didn't prove enough. In the end, it too was vanity.

No Amount of Education

Having acquired knowledge equivalent to multiple academic degrees, Solomon came to some sobering conclusions.[2] The first appears at the beginning of Ecclesiastes 1:15: "What is crooked cannot be straightened." The second observation immediately follows: "What is lacking cannot be counted." And then verse 18 adds: "in much wisdom there is much grief, and increasing knowledge results in increasing pain."

Solomon would contend that "a thief with a Ph.D. is still a thief." Educated thieves still steal—they just pull off more complicated heists. The crooked cannot be made straight merely through schooling. In other words, no amount of knowledge will make an immoral person moral. No amount of education will enable a selfish person to become generous or make a mean person kind. It cannot turn a liar honest or rid an impure mind of the desire for pornography. That was Solomon's first conclusion.

Next he discovered that education does not make something of nothing. If a void exists in a person's life, education alone will not fill it. Take one lonely person, add the best education the world can offer, and what do you get? A well-educated lonely person. No amount of finite reasoning can change the circumstances of our life. We cannot alter what is unjust or bring perfection out of imperfection through the aid of our finite minds. By ourselves, we cannot correct the ills and tragedies of this life.

Then Solomon will add, "Hey! Knowing more will just increase your pain. You will discover pain you never knew existed." It's the agony of knowing that something is wrong but not being in a position to stop it. The pain of realizing that not all your neat little answers about life are so neat after all. The torment of being confused by conflicting philosophies and worldviews and cultures. And most of all, the pain of accountability and decision, now that you know.

But here's the zinger and the last observation we'll take a look at. Solomon gets down to the nitty-gritty in chapter 2. There in verses 14 and 15 we find these vivid words: "The wise man's eyes are in his head, but the fool walks in darkness. And yet I know that one fate befalls them both. Then I said to myself, 'As is the fate of the fool, it will also befall me. Why then have I been extremely wise?'" Wise men bite the dust, and so do fools. The lights go out for both. No matter how far up the ladder of intellectual pursuit we have climbed, we will die and be forgotten (verse 16). No amount of schooling or booksmarts will get you past the casket.[3]

Now, we need to make one thing perfectly clear. Solomon is not anti-wisdom or bad-mouthing education. He's not rejecting careful, deep, creative thinking or the pursuit of knowledge. In fact, he acknowledges that wisdom and knowledge have some definite advantages, as we see in his illustration of a man chopping down a tree (Eccl. 10:10). If the man is smart, he will sharpen the axe. Otherwise he will have to use more strength. That is simply using wisdom to one's practical advantage. Wisdom can ensure success and help one foresee problems. But it is not the answer to the meaning of life. Knowledge apart from God is an empty pursuit.

Spiritual IQ

Daniel Goleman's best-selling book *Emotional Intelligence: Why It Can Matter More Than IQ*[4] brings a contemporary twist to Solomon's observations. It's straight evolutionary sociobiology, but it has some real gems stuck in there about how our brain works. Goleman's bottom line is that it takes more than academic smarts to be a success in life. One's IQ contributes only 20 percent of the factors that determine success. A full 80 percent derives from other factors, one of which is "emotional intelligence." There's an emotional IQ behind our intelligence IQ that can separate the stars from the average performer.

Solomon would say it this way: A spiritual IQ behind our intelligence IQ can divide those who live *above the sun* from those who live *under the sun*. This inner quality places a knowledge of God and a relationship with Him before anything else.

The ancient king would describe such a spiritual IQ as a well-driven nail to hang our intellects on. "God gives those who please Him wisdom, knowledge, and joy" (Eccl. 2:26, TLB). Do you know what it means to please the Lord? Please Him in a way that opens to you wisdom and knowledge with joy? I believe Solomon was thinking back on his own experience when he wrote these words. Remember that night in Gibeon? As a young king he yearned for wisdom and understanding so he could accomplish the work God had given him to do. He longed for a quick mind, a large heart. Then one night the Lord appeared to Solomon in a dream and said, "Ask what you wish me to give you" (1 Kings 3:5).

In answer Solomon prayed: "Thou hast made Thy servant king, . . . yet I am but a little child; I do not know how to go out or come in. . . . So give Thy servant an understanding heart to judge Thy people to discern between good and evil. For who is able to judge this great people of Thine?" (1 Kings 3:7-9). Remember how God felt about that prayer? "It was pleasing in the sight of the Lord that Solomon had asked this thing" (verse 10).

Solomon's prayer revealed his humility and his strong desire to honor God in everything. He realized that without divine aid he was as helpless as a little child. A sense of humility and reverence before Him and a grasp of our own limitations pleases the Lord. Ellen White tells us that "Solomon was never so rich or so wise or so truly great as when he confessed, 'I am but a little child: I know not how to go out or come in.'"[5]

The pursuit of knowledge comes down to spiritual attitude, a spiritual IQ. The person who begins his or her quest for knowledge with a basic trust in God is given wisdom and knowledge with joy. True wisdom begins when we acknowledge our Maker and believe in Him, trust in Him. "The fear of the Lord is the beginning of wisdom, and the knowledge of the Holy One is understanding," Solomon writes in Proverbs 9:10. Anything less is simply busywork in the classroom we call life.

Somewhere along the way Solomon's brain overran his heart, and he lost his sense of humility and reverence. Like him, many of us will never come to God until we have emptied ourselves of earthly wisdom—until we have done everything our minds tell us to do and see the emptiness of it all. Many of us are waiting until we understand everything about redemption or our Christian responsibility before we give our hearts fully to God in surrendered obedience. Rather than trusting God, we try by human wisdom to explain God's Word away. As Solomon implies at the end of his book, "the writing of many books is endless, and excessive devotion to books is wearing to the body" (Eccl. 12:12). We press on and on for answers, ever studying, but never coming to a knowledge of truth. Like the Room of Answers in Jonathan Swift's satire *Gulliver's Travels,* the university of life has myriads of rooms in which everyone is busy seeking answers, pursuing the meaning of life. But cobwebs cover the door to the Room of Answers.

In his book *When All You've Ever Wanted Isn't Enough* Rabbi Kushner refers to a Jewish tradition of the "holy fool." They are simple, uneducated, unsophisticated persons who serve God spontaneously and enthusiastically without stopping to think about what they are doing. Such service to God is especially beloved because "no intellectual barriers come between him and his God."[6]

But God doesn't want "holy fools," nor does He want intellectual barriers. What He desires is men and women who know and love Him and who expand their minds to reach their fullest potential for His glory. We have a choice as to whether we will seek wisdom and knowledge with joy, or wisdom and knowledge with grief. Wisdom and knowledge with eternity on the horizon, or wisdom and knowledge *under the sun,* with only the grave as our future.

In addition, God wants us to realize that only a relationship with Him can straighten what is crooked in our lives. Only a relationship with Him can fill in where we're empty or make up for some lack. It alone can bring hope or perspective along with the grief that increased knowledge so often brings.

Wiring for Eternity

"God gives those who please him wisdom, knowledge, and joy" (Eccl. 2:26, TLB). "The knowledge of the Holy One is understanding" (Prov. 9:10). The true pursuit of wisdom and knowledge comes down to how our spiritual brains are wired! We need an *above the sun* education. A relationship with God. The kind of thing Jesus spoke to Nicodemus about: "Are you the teacher of Israel, and do not understand these things?" (John 3:10). But, Ellen White tells us, "the truth as it is in Jesus can be experienced, but never explained."[7]

One of the interesting points in *Newsweek's* article on the brain is a graph that outlines what researchers call the windows of opportunity for things such as motor development, emotional control, vision, social attachment, vocabulary, second language, math/logic, and music. If you sew a kitten's eye shut, will the kitten be blind forever when you do reopen the eye? The answer is yes! The neural wiring will not take place in the visual cortex for that eye. If you have had your spiritual eye sewn shut, will you be spiritually blind forever? Here, fortunately, the answer is no! The windows of opportunity remain throughout life—although with diminishing potential for overall impact on life.

How's your brain wired? Are you wired for information and facts or for a relationship with the living God of heaven? Have you experienced the truth as it is in Jesus?

----

[1] Sharon Begely, "Your Child's Brain," *Newsweek,* Feb. 19, 1996, pp. 55-62.

[2] See James T. Draper, Jr., *Ecclesiastes: The Life Without God* (Wheaton, Ill.: Tyndale House Publishers, 1981), pp. 15-22; E. Young, *The Meaning of Life,* pp. 77, 78, 89.

[3] Wisdom also brings short-lived gratitude, such as the poor man, who by his wisdom and ingenuity delivered a city from destruction (Eccl. 9:13-18). He fooled the enemy and saved the city, but no one remembered him. The pursuit of wisdom leads us to the emptiness of trusting in the public praise of other people. Those people who praise us the most will be the first to criticize us. See Draper, p. 19.

[4] Daniel Goleman, *Emotional Intelligence: Why It Means More Than IQ* (New York: Bantam Books, 1995). Goleman writes for the New York *Times* and is a former senior editor of *Psychology Today.*

[5] E. G. White, *Prophets and Kings,* p. 30.

[6] Harold Kushner, *When All You've Ever Wanted Isn't Enough* (New York: Pocket Books, 1986), p. 108.

[7] White, *Christ's Object Lessons* (Washington, D.C.: Review and Herald Pub. Assn., 1900), p. 129.

6

WHEN ALL YOU'VE EVER
WANTED ISN'T ENOUGH

He who loves money will not be satisfied with money,
> *but he who loves abundance with its income.*
This too is vanity.
When good things increase, those who consume them increase.
So what is the advantage to their owners except to look on?
The sleep of the working man is pleasant, whether he eats
> *little or much.*
But the full stomach of the rich man does not allow him to sleep.
There is a grievous evil which I have seen under the sun:
> *riches being hoarded by their owner to his hurt.*
When those riches were lost through bad investment and
> *he had fathered a son,*
> *then there was nothing to support him.*
As he had come naked from his mother's womb, so will he return as
> *he came.*
He will take nothing from the fruit of his labor that he can
> *carry in his hand.*
And this also is a grievous evil—exactly as a man is born,
> *thus will he die.*
So, what is the advantage to him who toils for the wind?
Throughout his life he also eats in darkness with great
> *vexation, sickness and anger.*
Here is what I have seen to be good and fitting:

to eat, to drink and enjoy oneself in all one's labor in which
he toils under the sun
during the few years of his life which God has given him;
for this is his reward.
Furthermore, as for every man to whom God has given
riches and wealth,
He has also empowered him to eat from them and to receive
his reward and rejoice in his labor;
this is the gift of God.
For he will not often consider the years of his life,
because God keeps him occupied with the gladness of his heart.
—Ecclesiastes 5:10-20

Existentialist philosopher Albert Camus wrote a short story of a dry-goods merchant named Marcel who lived in a small village and married a beautiful girl. Marcel often went on trips to sell his wools and silks, but his wife, Janine, stayed home, never leaving the village. Finally he convinced her to accompany him on a trip into the city. He had several appointments that first afternoon and was so preoccupied with seeing the important merchants that Janine felt left behind, wishing she were home and thinking about their 25 years of marriage.

For some reason all the men she encountered along the streets and in the shops caused her to remember a lustful dream she had had since she was a young girl. Now she had the opportunity to fulfill her sensual dream, but she feared what her husband would do if he discovered her unfaithfulness. So instead of acting out her impulse, she wandered the streets in ambivalence until he finished his business. They had a lovely dinner together and walked around a bit. Then they went up to their room and got into bed. Marcel fell asleep quickly, but Janine could not. Tossing and turning, she again remembered her dream. Finally, Camus writes, Janine arose from bed, dressed, walked out into the night, and indulged her fantasy.

Early the next morning she returned quietly, undressed, and got back into bed with her unknowing husband. Then she began to sob, crying so loudly that she woke her husband. "What's the matter?" Marcel asked.

"It's nothing, dear," she replied. "It's nothing."[1] And that was the end of the story. It is typical of the way *under the sun* stories told by existentialists conclude. But there is an *above the sun* footnote that we can add: "The loneliest day in our lives is when we experience our wildest dreams and come away empty."[2]

Nothing could be more true, says Solomon, for the kind of dreams money, wealth, and materialism bring to a life lived strictly *under the sun.* The most dangerous love affair any man or woman will ever experience in this life is one with money. Money is a deceitful object of desire, because it can never deliver what it promises. If we could have absolutely everything we ever imagined or dreamed of, it still wouldn't be enough. The man or woman with eternity in his or her heart needs more satisfying nourishment than this world can provide.

Solomon should know. When he writes about the emptiness of materialism, he knows what he's talking about. He was one of those "fat cats," with an estimated $25 million annual income in gold alone. The man's spread included parks, zoos, lavish resorts, riding stables, gold drinking cups, plush living quarters, fancy clothes, exotic foods—you name it! He was affluence personified. You and I, honestly, cannot comprehend the immensity of Solomon's wealth. Neither could the queen of Sheba. Intrigued by his "press releases," she traveled up from Ethiopia to check it out for herself.

When you read the account of her visit in 1 Kings 10, you find her "blown away." "She was breathless and overcome," it says in *The Amplified Bible* (verse 5). Solomon's wisdom and wealth overwhelmed her! "I wasn't told half of it," she exclaimed (see verse 7, Amplified). Although she was acquainted with elegance and enjoyed enormous wealth herself, she was speechless after seeing his court. The luxury and beauty that dripped from Solomon's kingdom stunned her. She responded to his wealth and power in the only way she knew how: by giving him more. The queen presented him with 120 talents of gold—roughly $3.5 million in today's currency—and a generous cache of spices and precious stones.

Solomon knew both the good side and the down side of material possessions. But before we see what he has to say, I want to make something very clear. Biblical references to the rich do not always refer to people with a lot of money. Many times Scripture has in mind a person who lives for wealth and material possessions. A poor man or woman might also fit that category. Ecclesiastes speaks to anyone with the urge to acquire more. It does not matter whether we are struggling to pay bills and desire more, or whether we have money in the bank and crave still more.

A Real Heartbreaker

Solomon knew the subject of wealth as did few others. "He who loves money will not be satisfied with money, nor he who loves abundance with its income" (Eccl. 5:10). Before we go any further, observe that the word Solomon uses is "love"—not "possesses." It is no sin to have money, but money is not neutral. It breeds dissatisfaction. The money-hungry never have enough. Those who love money will never reach the level of personal satisfaction. They will never know the day when they will lean back, smile contentedly, and sigh, "That's plenty. I have enough." "How much does it take to satisfy us? A little bit more than we have!"[3] It's amazing, isn't it? If advertisers are right, we have a lot to feel discontent about. We don't have enough possessions, and we don't have them soon enough or up-to-date enough. Advertising equates fulfillment with wearing the right kind of clothes, driving the right kind of car, drinking the right kind of beverage. As Chuck Swindoll says, "Money can buy tons of comfort, but not an ounce of contentment."[4]

Second, money brings frustration. "When good things increase, those who consume them increase. So what is the advantage to their owners except to look on? The sleep of the working man is pleasant, whether he eats little or much. But the full stomach of the rich man does not allow him to sleep" (Eccl. 5:11, 12). *The Living Bible* puts verse 11: "The more you have, the more you spend, right up to the limits of your income, so what is the advantage of wealth—except perhaps to watch it as it runs through your fingers!" How often we've seen that occur. Spending right up to the limit of our income and . . . watching it go . . . to taxes, late fees, service charges, interest rates, maintenance contracts, attorneys, accountants, insurance premiums, and alarm systems. The list could go on endlessly!

And don't forget anxiety and sleepless nights. Our family was reminded of some of these things when we purchased a shiny new car. We had been driving an old silver-colored Volkswagen Jetta. After 16 years no one cared any longer what it looked like or what happened to it. In fact, toward the end I was fixing it every few weeks and found myself wishing someone would run into it. Then, at least, I would have some money to pay taxes on a new one. Anyway, you know what I found myself saying the day I drove my new car home? "I'm going to keep this car clean and shining. I'm going to wash and wax it regularly and keep the inside trash-free. I'm going to talk to the guys about their feet on the seat backs, writing their initials on steamed windows, and where they park their bikes in the garage." I knew my boys had the same idea when one of them commented, "No one should put chewing gum in the trash pockets, right, Daddy?"

People with possessions have a lot on their minds. Life then gets complicated, risky, and stressful. Remember Shirley, our friend from Florida who got wiped out by Hurricane Andrew? She told us that now whenever she walks into a home, especially a new and rather ritzy place, she doesn't see the fancy wallpaper or window trim or lighting or furniture. She sees every house now as just rafters. Shirley knows how quickly it can come down to just that— or in her case, nothing at all.

And you can't take it with you! That's how Solomon sums it up in verse 16: "This also is a grievous evil—exactly as a man is born, thus will he die. So, what is the advantage to him who toils for the wind?" People can make all the money they want and amass all the material possessions they can, but they will not take one penny with them beyond death. No U-Haul trailers follow the hearse to the graveside. Solomon understood the folly of his Egyptian contemporaries. In the end you need something more that money just can't buy—the living God.

He Keeps Us Occupied

Stuart Peters was one of my best friends ever! Never have I been as close to someone before or since. We were both newcomers to a small church in the metropolitan Washington, D.C., area. I was fresh out of seminary on my first assignment and 25 years old. Stu was fresh out of the baptistry following an evangelistic crusade held just before my arrival—and old enough to be my dad. When we met, something just clicked. Maybe it was my youthfulness of age and his youthfulness of Christian experience. Whatever, we became fast friends who shared a vision for God and worked together for seven years building up that small church into a thriving Adventist congregation.

Stu was young in the Lord but pretty experienced with life lived *under the sun*. In fact, the IRS was after him, and his business had gone into receivership. Here was a man who had had his day in the sun but was now living on a shoestring and driving his late father's old beat-up car. My friend was philosophical about it, though. The stress and anxiety lay behind him as he focused on eternal values. When he would pick me up in that old car on our way for Bible studies, he would often quip that Jesus had not been into material things, and that he had a hard time now visualizing himself driving up for a Bible study in the fancy Cadillacs he used to drive. But God has a way of changing our view of things. In time Stu's business got back on track. God's increasing blessings proved the truth of Malachi's promise for faithfulness in tithes and offerings.

I can still remember the day vividly. I had stepped out the front door of our church knowing Stu would be arriving any minute to pick me up for a Bible study. As I walked out into the parking lot, I watched a shiny two-toned silver Cadillac Seville with dark windows pull up beside me. The electric window rolled down smartly. And there sat Stu. He just looked at me with a grin and said, "Get in, or we'll be late." He knew exactly what I was thinking. Silently we drove around the parking lot and out onto the street. But—but he couldn't bear it. So he pulled over to the curb and just blurted it out. "Larry, I can't help it God blesses me!" As we sat there, he shared a story I already knew. God was restoring his fortunes! During the next few years I watched my friend's generosity literally bless people and bless God's church. Many times I watched him pull a roll of $100 bills out of his pocket and peel them off for some person in need, some church project. "I can't help it God blesses me! Should I live like He doesn't? Should I not enjoy or celebrate His goodness?"

That's what our passage is all about. Solomon points us to another view of money and material things. "Here is what I have seen to be good and fitting: to eat, to drink and enjoy oneself in all one's labor in which he toils under the sun during the few years of his life which God has given him; for this is his reward. Furthermore, as for every man to whom God has given riches and wealth, He has also empowered him to eat from them and to receive his reward and rejoice in his labor; this is the gift of God. For he will not often consider the years of his life, because God keeps him occupied with the gladness of his heart" (verses 18-20).

Ecclesiastes presents money as a blessing from God, a means of enhancing our relationship with Him and helping those around us. It's all right for us to enjoy the blessings that freely come our way. In fact, Solomon calls it good and beautiful to be able to enjoy the rather worldly things obtainable through money. Eating and drinking has an unabashedly sensual and earthly character to it. It is expressive of joy, satisfaction, and companionship. Solomon is talking about the dinner out at the Olive Garden, the new blouse to enhance your beauty, your vacation in Canada, the new CD in your collection, the cleaner, more dependable car, the quiet home outside of town, the air-conditioning on blistering hot days. He's speaking about enjoying life. Like our family will often do on a Saturday night when we will buy some chips, make some pizza, and just sit around enjoying something special together. God meant the blessings of life to be enjoyed and shared and lived and celebrated. Scripture unashamedly holds out the positive side of money and material blessings as realities we can freely rejoice in and enjoy.[5]

Let's be sure we understand what Solomon is saying and not misconstrue it, though. It is no evangelical good-life theology such as we hear today. Wealth in a secular context will certainly lead to misery. But here is the possibility of wealth combined with the power to enjoy it—even the encouragement to enjoy it. The secular-minded person assumes that the two invariably go together—wealth and enjoyment, but Solomon separates them. Here is where he brings God into the picture. Being rich involves more than having money. You need to be able to enjoy material things, but you can enjoy them only in a certain context—a relationship with God. God both gives wealth and empowers us to enjoy it.

Solomon rejects our seeking material things as ends in themselves, as something to enjoy in themselves or as a worthwhile life goal. Rather we are to rejoice and enjoy them, because *God* has graciously given them to us. The kind of enjoyment of life that Solomon has in mind is in reality celebrating God. As we eat and drink and fill up our senses we keep God's gracious goodness in mind and praise Him. Our laughing and joyfulness flow from the inner chambers of hearts worshiping God. Material things become tangible evidences of His goodness and love.

An older pastor friend of mine surprised me once with an incredible unexpected offer. "My wife and I have a condo in the resort town of Winter Park, Colorado," he stated, "and we want you to take your family there for a week. Free!"

"What?" I exclaimed. And then he told me the story of how, when he was a young pastor with a young family and living on a shoestring budget, his next-door neighbor, who wasn't a Seventh-day Adventist, surprised him with a wonderful gift. The man had won a sweepstakes that included two weeks in a resort condo. "We've had our days of fun in life," the older man said. "We only need a week. Why don't you pack your family up and take them for the second week?" My pastor friend said it was a dream come true. They barely had the money to drive the distance, and took all their own food along. But it was the blessing their struggling family needed right then. Following that weeklong gift, my friend and his wife made a vow. If they were ever able to return that favor to some other denominational employee family, they would. God heard that dream and blessed. Now he was passing that offer on to my family of four boys between the ages of 3 and 11. How did he know we had no money and hadn't ever really gone anywhere on a family vacation?

Those seven days in Winter Park proved the blessing my friend intended—and more! During that week we often remembered and spoke of our gracious benefactor—why he thought of us, what he had given us. We couldn't help it! All around the condo were pictures and books and games and objects that pointed to him and his interests or had his name inscribed on them. Never once during that week did we think that condo was ours. Nor did we want to keep it. Holding it loosely but enjoying it freely, we were spontaneously grateful. And when it was time to go home, we rejoiced in what we'd had for that short time. Our family will never forget that week, nor will we ever forget the one who gave it to us.

So it is with God! The house we live in is His house. The car we drive is His car. The garden we plant is His. And so is the chocolate mousse pie at the Olive Garden. We are only temporary stewards of things that belong to Another. When we enjoy the things He lends us, we think of Him and His love. Material things are tangible evidences of His goodness and love enjoyed for what they are—gifts! But in the end, it is He that we really enjoy. The only way our possessions or blessings can bring meaning is when we look past them to the One who has provided.

69

Have you ever touched or played a $2 million musical instrument? My wife, Kathie, was negotiating the sale of a violin and the possible purchase of another at Chicago's prestigious Bein and Fushi. As I talked with the salesperson, somehow we got on the topic of the unique wood characteristics found in some instruments.

"Let me show you something," he said as he walked into the vault where the instruments were kept. He returned with a delicate violin that had what looked like a crack along the back. "It's a mineral trace in the wood," he said. "Looks like a crack, but it's not!" he said adamantly.

Then I asked him what kind of violin it was. "Stradivarius. One of his earliest ones. We have it on sale for $2 million." Imagine my amazement!

"May my wife play it?" I asked cautiously.

"Sure!" And so Kathie spent a half hour or so playing a $2 million instrument. On our way home we kept looking at each other and thinking of the opportunity we had just had. It reminded us so much of life. Like the Strad, which she played and enjoyed for a few brief moments and then returned to its owner, material blessings are not ours, but His as we play and enjoy them in the moment we call life.

I think of David sitting before the Lord in speechless awe. "Who am I, O Lord God, and what is my house that thou hast brought me this far?" (1 Chron. 17:16). When we really begin to see how great and lovely God is and how good He has been to us, we rise up in praise. We're humbled. We are occupied with Him and not the things He gives us to enjoy.

Everything is a gift. When we are aware of that fact, it frees us from a possessive and anxious spirit. This is what our money-mad society so desperately needs—to be delivered from the bewitching desire to hold on to what we have and to acquire even more. To escape the worry and energy and the troubles involved in keeping up or getting ahead.

Sand Castles

In his book *And the Angels Were Silent* Max Lucado tells about the builders of two castles. The one is a little boy on the beach. The sun is hot and the air salty. The rhythmic waves rush up on the sand. On his knees the child scoops and packs the sand with plastic shovels in a bright red bucket. Then he upends the bucket on the surface and lifts it. To the delight of the little architect, he creates a castle tower. All afternoon he will work spooning out the moat and packing the walls. Bottle tops will be sentries, and popsicle sticks will be bridges.

The other castle builder is an adult man. There in the big city, with busy streets rumbling with traffic, he sits in his office. At his desk he shuffles papers into stacks and delegates assignments. He cradles the phone and punches the keyboard with his fingers. Numbers get juggled and contracts signed, and much to his delight, he makes a profit. All his life he will work, formulating plans and forecasting the future. Annuities will be sentries. Capital gains will be bridges. The man builds an empire.

The two builders of two castles have much in common. Diligent and determined, they make something out of nothing. And for both the tide will rise and the end will come. Yet that is where the similarities end. For the boy sees the end of his creation, while the man ignores it. Watch the boy as the dusk approaches and each wave slaps an inch closer to his castle. He doesn't panic, nor is he surprised at the advance of the surging waves. Soon they will wash away his castle.

The man, however, remains oblivious to the fate of all that he has done even though constant reminders surround him. Days come and go. Seasons ebb and flow. Every sunrise that becomes a sunset whispers, "Time will take your castles."

So one is prepared and one isn't. One is peaceful while the other panics. As the waves near, the child jumps to his feet and begins to clap. He feels no sorrow, no fear or regret. When the great breaker

71

crashes into his castle and sucks his masterpiece into the sea, he smiles, picks up his shovels, takes his father's hand, and goes home. The grown-up, however, is not so wise. As the wave of years collapse his castle, he is terrified. Hovering over the sandy monument to protect it, he tries to block the waves from the walls he has made. "It's my castle," he protests. But finally the cliff of water mounts high above the man and his little empire and he is left on his knees, clutching sandy handfuls of yesterday. If only he had known. If only he had listened.[6]

"The loneliest day in our lives is when we experience our wildest dreams and come away empty." Money is a deceitful object of desire, because it can never deliver what it promises. It's a fickle lover, and its accumulation not a worthy life goal. But the living God of heaven does not disappoint. He will never leave us empty. Instead, He empowers us to enjoy what He graciously gives.

Being rich involves a lot more than making more money. There is knowing God's love and celebrating His goodness!

---

[1] Albert Camus, "The Adulterous Woman," in his *Exile and the Kingdom* (New York: Alfred A. Knopf, 1963), pp. 3-33.

[2] E. Young, *The Meaning of Life*, p. 105.

[3] C. Swindoll, *Living on the Ragged Edge*, p. 163.

[4] *Ibid.*

[5] See Richard J. Foster, *Money, Sex, and Power: The Challenge of the Disciplined Life* (New York: Harper and Row, 1985), pp. 19-87.

[6] Max Lucado, *And the Angels Were Silent* (Portland, Oreg.: Multnomah, 1992), pp. 127-129.

HONEY, I SHRUNK THE KIDS! NO, IT WAS GOD!

Guard your steps as you go to the house of God,
*   and draw near to listen rather than to offer the sacrifice of fools;*
*   for they do not know they are doing evil.*
Do not be hasty in word or impulsive in thought to bring up
*   a matter in the presence of God.*
For God is in heaven and you are on earth;
*   therefore let your words be few.*
For the dream comes through much effort, and the voice of
*   a fool through many words.*
When you make a vow to God, do not be late in paying it,
*   for He takes no delight in fools.*
Pay what you vow!
It is better that you should not vow than that you should
*   vow and not pay.*
Do not let your speech cause you to sin and do not say in
*   the presence of the messenger of God that it was a mistake.*
Why should God be angry on account of your voice and destroy
*   the work of your hands?*
For in many dreams and in many words there is emptiness.
Rather, fear God.

                              —Ecclesiastes 5:1-7

C an you imagine ants bigger than cars? Or grass about 20 feet high? What would it be like to have a raindrop the size of a 10-gallon bucket fall on you? Or to curl up inside a Lego to keep safe as you sleep? How about hanging on to a Cheerio as a life preserver so you won't drown in a bowl of milk? All the while hoping your father doesn't pick you up in the next spoonful and eat you alive? Can you imagine standing on the kitchen table yelling at the top of your voice, "I'm here, I'm here," but you're so small no one can see you unless they have a magnifying glass? *Honey, I Shrunk the Kids!* is one of those recklessly inane Walt Disney comedies about a preoccupied scientist father who inadvertently shrinks his kids with the scientific device he invented to compress objects.

At first he doesn't know that his invention really works, or that his kids are now just tiny quarter-inch beings on the floor. As he walks across the room, they run for their lives. When he sweeps up the floor, they get whisked into a dustpan and thrown out with the trash. Once it dawns on him what has happened, he searches frantically to find them. Using a magnifying glass, he explores his workroom inch by inch, and then the yard. But the kids are too small. Even as they stand on the kitchen table yelling, "We're here! We're here!" he doesn't see them, even though his heart aches to find them.

When I read the words from Ecclesiastes at the beginning of this chapter, it makes me think of how we push God down in our thinking. How we inadvertently shrink Him in our eyes. God stands right there before us, passionately crying, "I'm here! I'm here!" But we don't see or hear Him, because He's not big enough to really capture our attention or our hearts! Our mind and our hearts are elsewhere.

"Guard your steps as you go to the house of God" (Eccl. 5:1) Solomon declares. In other words, when you go into the house of God, go in on tiptoe! Approach God with care. Now, why would Solomon say that? Because he too had inadvertently shrunk God in his sight. He was too busy doing his own thing—partying, researching for that next degree, making money and acquiring more. Busy with a host of things *under the sun,* so that God became smaller and smaller in his thinking. Here Solomon confesses that he had even been busy "doing church." He had simply let himself get caught up in what millions are doing today to find meaning in life: attending church, trying religion, being religious. But his inner private world never equaled his public worship.

The church Solomon attended would have been considered the "mainstream Seventh-day Adventist remnant" congregation of his time. It was the Temple of Jerusalem. And Solomon not only attended—he had built it. He showed up at all the services and participated in all the feasts. Probably he knew all the priests by their first names. Externally faithful in every way as far as his religious community was concerned, he paid tithe, sang the hymns, wore the right clothes, kept the Sabbath, and didn't eat at Red Lobster. Sometimes he preached a sermon here or there. Hey! He was a real pew warmer. We'd call him a "cultural Adventist." Because he was simply playing church, God wasn't really all that big in his eyes. This too was empty, meaningless vanity.

Bringing God Up to Size

Once Solomon realized he had shrunk God, he began the frantic search to find Him. In the process he realized that some things needed to change in his thinking. He came to understand that he needed a different attitude if God were to come back up to size for him again. So we find three well-driven nails to hang our relationship with God on. They secure our worship and perspectives of Him.

The first nail appears in verse 1: "Guard your steps as you go to the house of God, and draw near to listen rather than to offer the sacrifice of fools; for they do not know they are doing evil" (Eccl. 5:1). Go into God's presence on tiptoe, Solomon says. Approach Him with care and listening ears and responsive hearts. Don't just go through the motions, because it's your Adventist routine or because others do it. You mustn't approach Him as you would show up at just any other place just to hear, to sit, to talk, to leave. And don't come in a casual, unprepared manner. Make sure your heart is in your actions. Otherwise you'll be offering the sacrifice of fools. And what is that? Here's how Ed Young puts it:

"It is the kind of worship that never shows itself in our daily lives. A fool gives God the sacrifice of singing and praying and giving and sharing, and then goes out and lives as he pleases. The fool's worship never changes him. When we go through the motions of devotions and church and worship and Christianity, and our hearts remain the same, we have offered the sacrifice of fools." [1]

The command to bring listening ears suggests that God may speak. He might reveal His presence. So we need to prepare, to be still, to be quiet enough to hear. Our hearts need to participate. Listening ears also suggest our readiness to obey. What is Solomon telling us? That if we draw near and listen well, God will become more important to us. But if we don't, He'll shrink in our eyes and we won't be able to see Him.

Verses 2 and 3 and the first part of verse 7 contain Solomon's second nail: "Do not be hasty in word or impulsive in thought to bring up a matter in the presence of God. For God is in heaven and you are on earth; therefore let your words be few. For the dream comes through much effort, and the voice of a fool through many words. . . . For in many dreams and in many words there is emptiness" (Eccl. 5:2-7).

Daydreaming is one of the things Solomon has in mind in these verses. In his commentary on Ecclesiastes Derek Kidner says: "The dreams appear to be daydreams, reducing worship to verbal doodling." It's easy to "doodle" [2] our way through a worship service as we let our dream world take us from one imaginary vista to another: last summer's vacation, that new vehicle you're going to buy, the needs of the kids, who's coming over for Sabbath dinner, or the roast that's burning because church service is running late. Only as we keep our thoughts focused will God become more important to us.

But I believe Solomon has still another thought in mind here. "Do not be hasty in word or impulsive in thought to bring up a matter in the presence of God. For God is in heaven and you are on earth; therefore let your words be few" (Eccl. 5:2). What does he mean? Many understand this to refer to prayer. The kind of prayer Larry Crabb talks about in his book *Finding God,*[3] in which feeling better or solving some problem or getting something has become more important to us than seeking God. Until our passion for finding God grows deeper than any other passion, we will just be asking for a lot of things. We will be hasty in word and impulsive in thought when coming before God.

I believe, however, that Solomon may also be referring to our tendency to evaluate and comment on everything that we experience while "doing church." All those silent things we say to ourselves in our heart, or whisper to another worshiper, or gossip about during Sabbath afternoon dinner. Things like: "This is boring!" "I'm not getting fed." "They sang that out of tune." "Why didn't the sound man . . . ?" "We're running late again." "The organ's too loud." "I wish the pulpit was bigger." "Nobody said hello to me." "Who's that big-eared fellow with that fancy-dressed gal?" "That's the tenth time the preacher said 'uh' in his sermon." "This pew is uncomfortable." "I don't know this song."

We are too hasty in our words and impulsive in our thinking toward other worshipers, those leading out in worship, what we're hearing—even God, Scripture, the standards of the church, the writings of Ellen G. White, the content of the message, all the other things that could be done. It all mirrors our consumer-oriented generation.

But Solomon will say, "Be careful what you think and say in your heart. For when you are busy evaluating everything, God shrinks in our eyes. We're not able to gain the blessing that is there for us to receive. But when we watch the kinds of things that go on in our heart and the attitudes we express, God will become bigger in our eyes. Remember, God is in heaven, and we are on earth. That is a statement of perspective, not distance. It is *we* who are ultimately critiqued, not God."

The third nail has to do with keeping our commitments: "When

77

you make a vow to God, do not be late in paying it, for He takes no delight in fools. Pay what you vow! It is better that you should not vow than that you should vow and not pay. Do not let your speech cause you to sin and do not say in the presence of the messenger of God that it was a mistake. Why should God be angry on account of your voice and destroy the work of your hands?" (Eccl. 5:4-6).

According to Chuck Swindoll, "these are some of the most over-looked words in all of Scripture—especially so in our day of shallow roots and superficial commitments."[4] We would much rather bail out than follow through on things when they get tough or boring. But Solomon has more in mind here than finances.

Consider for a moment some of the promises we've made to God. No doubt some of us have made a commitment to meet with God every morning at 6:15 to pray for the Holy Spirit. We've promised to spend more time with our family—to give them top-priority attention. Years ago, perhaps, we made a vow at the altar with the person we loved, in which we said we would be faithful for the rest of our life. Or stood before God's people with a baby in arm and affirmed our desire to rear that child God's way. Maybe we lay back in the waters of baptism dedicating ourselves to a God-honoring life, or heard God's Word address the subject of purity and promised ourselves and God to remain morally pure for our marriage partner.

I wonder too how many times the Lord has heard prayers like these? "Oh, God, if You'll get me out of this tight place, I'm Yours from now on." Or "Lord, if You'll just help me do this thing, I'm going to start being a better father or being a better husband or start going to church or telling the truth." How many times do we leave worship or our personal devotions with a burning desire to do some specific thing—tell someone we're sorry, let someone know we forgive them, begin returning a faithful tithe, let God take control of our life, make some wrong right—but let it fade away? We never follow through.

Solomon's words remind us that God takes our promises seri-ously. A promise made to God or before God becomes a covenant

78

with Him, and God does not regard such vows lightly. After all, He is the covenant-keeping God.

If we are serious about the commitments we've made, God will become more important in our life. But if our commitments become wishy-washy, then God diminishes in our sight. "Since you promised it, you should keep it," Solomon urges. He is not saying *if* you promise, but *when* we make a commitment. Our decisions are important to God. "God does not ignore or overlook our decisions."[5] Our integrity in these matters has to do with how big God really is in our lives. In the process, vows become the seed plot for God-honoring action.[6]

Three nails: Draw near and listen well. Be careful what you say in your heart. Keep your promises. If you do these things, God will not shrink in your life.

Stand in Awe

In Steven Spielberg's blockbuster movie *Jurassic Park* world-class paleontologist Allen Grant, who has devoted his life to the study of dinosaurs, suddenly comes face-to-face with real live prehistoric creatures. He falls to the ground, dumbstruck. The reason is obvious. It is one thing to piece together an informed but nonetheless imperfect image of dinosaurs by picking through fossils and bones, but to encounter an actual dinosaur firsthand—well, there can be no comparison. Later in the film, John Hammond, the wealthy impresario behind *Jurassic Park,* reflects on what motivated him to build his island menagerie: "I wanted to show people something that wasn't an illusion, something that was real, something they could see and touch and feel."

For many people, spirituality—doing church—amounts to picking through artifacts of faith that survive from long ago and far away. In that bygone era humans saw God, heard His voice, and experienced His awesome, at times terrible, power. But that was then. Today people generally regard those kinds of gripping encounters with the living God as extinct. They might as well be placed in the same category as *Jurassic Park:* fun to imagine, but unlikely to happen. Of course, if one ever did come face-to-face with God—with a God who wasn't an illusion, but Someone who was real, Someone you could see, touch, and feel—well, there could be no comparison. We'd likely fall down dumbstruck.[7]

Solomon speaks of standing in awe of God. Then he ends with the pregnant words: "Rather, fear God" (Eccl. 5:7). In other words, take Him seriously. But how? To fear God, you need to be in His presence, have a personal encounter with Him. Jacques Ellul makes the statement that "those who tremble in God's presence *are* in His presence."[8] As Elizabeth Browning said, "only he who sees takes off his shoes" in reverent fear.

After his encounter with God we find Job saying, "I have heard of Thee by the hearing of the ear; but now my eye sees Thee; therefore I retract, and I repent in dust and ashes" (Job 42:5, 6).

Jeremiah holds out the incredible reality: "Then you will call upon Me and come and pray to Me, and I will listen to you. And you will seek Me and find Me, when you search for Me with all your heart" (Jer. 29:12, 13).

How big is God to you? If He stood on the kitchen table passionately crying, "I'm here! I'm here!" would you see Him? Would you hear Him? Or has He become little in your sight? What would you need to do to bring Him up to full size in your heart? To have Him become so exalted in your thinking, so magnificent in your imagination, that *you* would be the little one who cries out from the kitchen table, "Lord! Lord! I'm here! I'm here!"?

We must intentionally, openly, honestly, quietly, in an attitude of reverence seek Him until we find Him. It took three days for Joseph and Mary to find Jesus once they lost track of Him. Although it may take time, if we persevere, He will become God to us once again.

---

[1] E. Young, *The Meaning of Life,* p. 119.

[2] Derek Kidner, *The Message of Ecclesiastes* (Downers Grove, Ill.: InterVarsity Press, 1976), p. 53.

[3] Larry Crabb, *Finding God* (Grand Rapids: Zondervan Pub. House, 1993), pp. 15-20.

[4] C. Swindoll, *Living on the Ragged Edge*, p. 153.

[5] *Ibid.*, p. 156.

[6] *Ibid.*, p. 154.

[7] Adapted from Willard D. Hendricks, *Exit Interviews: Revealing Stories of Why People Are Leaving the Church* (Chicago: Moody Press, 1993), p. 225.

[8] J. Ellul, *Reason for Being*, p. 276.

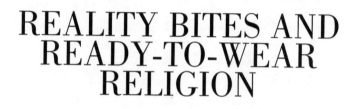

REALITY BITES AND READY-TO-WEAR RELIGION

Guard your steps as you go to the house of God,
and draw near to listen rather than to offer the sacrifice of fools;
for they do not know they are doing evil.
Do not be hasty in word or impulsive in thought to bring up
a matter in the presence of God.
For God is in heaven and you are on earth;
therefore let your words be few.
For the dream comes through much effort, and the voice of a fool
through many words.
When you make a vow to God, do not be late in paying it,
for He takes no delight in fools.
Pay what you vow!
It is better that you should not vow than that you should
vow and not pay.
Do not let your speech cause you to sin and do not say in
the presence of the messenger of God that it was a mistake.
Why should God be angry on account of your voice and destroy
the work of your hands?
For in many dreams and in many words there is emptiness.
Rather, fear God.

—Ecclesiastes 5:1-7

In his book *Reality Isn't What It Used to Be* Walter Truett Anderson tells of standing one day on a cliff overlooking the Pacific Ocean. A sea otter bobbed in the surf far below. The creature floated happily and busily on its back in the water, holding an abalone in its forepaws and cracking the abalone's shell with a rock. The waves gently rocked the creature. Although the water constantly moved the little animal this way and that, it seemed to pay no attention as it concentrated on its task. Then Anderson said, "I thought, how different from mine its experience of life must be, living in a medium in such flux and so unlike the hard ground on which I stood. But as I thought about it further, I realized that the medium in which I live is far more turbulent than anything the sea otter could ever conceive of—because as a human being, I bob about in a sea of symbols, an ocean of words."[1]

What Anderson has in mind is the collapse of belief taking place in our modern society. An ocean of words is creating a smorgasbord of diverse values and beliefs that no longer accept the permanent rightness of certain beliefs and values. The idea of objective or absolute or ultimate truth is fast becoming an archaism in our pluralistic American society. Self has become the source of truth and reality. We create reality with our words. As pragmatist Richard Rorty says, "anything can be made to look good or bad by being redescribed." Thus in literature and the media—indeed, even in politics—the lines between fantasy and fact are being erased.[2] Whether it is Hillary Rodham Clinton "lawyering the truth," as some say, about her involvement in Whitewater investments, or the O. J. Simpson defense team advancing other murder scenarios in order to create reasonable doubt, high-profile people characterize the trend of our age of words.

Solomon knew about words. He recognized what it was like to bob about in an ocean of them. In fact, he says, "In many dreams and in many words there is emptiness" (Eccl. 5:7). Later, in chapter 10, he adds, "The fool multiplies words. No man knows what will happen" (Eccl. 10:14). His point is that a lot of the words spoken in our world are just plain empty. All these meaningless words can cause a lot of moral and spiritual confusion. Thus Solomon grasped the power of words, how they shape our perception of reality and create reality for others as well as for ourselves. The ancient king knew about that, too. He did a little "reality creating" of his own. Referring to his writing of Ecclesiastes, he says, "The Preacher sought to find delightful words" (Eccl. 12:10). He was a master preacher, an orator who knew the power of words and a writer who understood what words can do. So he chose beautiful words. Creative words. Words that would catch attention, convince, and persuade.

Besides, Solomon adds, "Beyond this, my son, be warned: the writing of many books is endless, and excessive devotion to books is wearying to the body" (Eccl. 12:12). It's astonishing that he would write this at a time when books were rare. How much more then would his thoughts apply to our time? It is as if he wrote only yesterday. Solomon outlines a whole aspect of the world in our day— the overabundance of information, political discourse, books, newspapers, philosophical theories. In them we see the vanity of our whole culture and civilization. We're bobbing in an ocean of words, an ocean of beliefs and values.

Nothin' Until I Call 'Em

I want to make this more personal, more specific. Look at Ecclesiastes 5:6 where it says "do not sin with your mouth, or tell the preacher it was a mistake." This passage describes those who have changed their mind and are now trying to change the situation accordingly. In addition, they are attempting to alter the perception of others in the process. They seek to create a new reality. It was a mistake, they argue. Not an important vow to keep at all!

An old joke about three umpires takes us to the heart of what Solomon has in mind. They were sitting around drinking after a baseball game. One says, "There's balls and there's strikes, and I call 'em the way they are." Another responds, "There's balls and there's strikes, and I call 'em the way I see 'em." The third umpire adds, "There's balls and there's strikes, and they ain't *nothin'* until I call 'em."[3]

That brings us to one of the points Solomon makes here: our tendency to create our own reality, or describe reality as we see it or want it to be seen. Words express what we think, what we desire to have happen. For Solomon words are very important. God creates reality by what He says. I believe Solomon wrote Ecclesiastes with Genesis in hand. He had the truth ringing in his ears that God spoke and it was done, He commanded and it stood fast. His word is truth. In a lesser way we who are made in the image of God create reality too. We do so by what we say.

I want to note the relationship as well between words and dreams in Solomon's thinking. The concept of dreams here must stand for illusion, the trap of the unreal, the fictitious. They prevent us from seeing the reality we should be grasping. Such dreams are not just what we experience in our sleep, but those things that turn us from God, leading us to believe something else. Dreams characteristically get us to take them for reality.

Postmodern thinkers depict self as a dynamic, creative agent wielding words to get what it (the self) wants, always striving to transform things. Using language as a kind of gigantic crowbar, we attempt to roll away the stones of our contingencies, including sin and death.[4]

We experience it as Seventh-day Adventist Christians in the way we relate to Scripture and our remnant message. The competing interpretations of Scripture on certain points of theology or on those "hot potato" lifestyle issues confuse us and subtly cause us to think that the bottom line comes down to a sincere heart and believing what seems right to us. In essence Scripture becomes less important as we create a new reality. It happens too with the writings of Ellen G. White. We rationalize and explain so much away as culturalizations or specific rules for a bygone generation. Principled thinking is what we supposedly need.

Today it seems as though we can have whatever kind of God or religion we want. All we have to do is invent Him or decide what we want to believe or live by. Unfortunately many of us are mirroring society. A 1984 Gallup Poll revealed that 82 percent of Americans said that growing into a deeper relationship with God was important to them. But 60 percent of those polled rejected the idea that people should limit themselves to a single faith. And only 28 percent have a strong belief in objective, ultimate, or absolute truth.

We live in an age too of so-called values clarification. The history of the word "value" is significant. The avowed atheist Nietzsche coined the term as an alternative to an absolute right and an absolute wrong. Actually, values clarification in contemporary society is a misnomer. What we too often clarify are only individual wants and desires.

Reality Bites

The *CBS Evening News* with Dan Rather has had a feature called Reality Check. The segment will report some statement by a government official, politician, etc., and then, *bam!* a big rubber stamp comes across the screen that says "Reality Check." The news commentator then goes on to tell the other side of the story, seeking to set the facts straight.

Solomon calls us to a reality check. He assumes God has something to say. That there is a rightful and truthful word from the Lord. Notice what he states in chapter 12: "The Preacher sought to find delightful words and to write words of truth correctly" (verse 10). He sought creative, captivating words, convincing words. Persuasive words. But he wanted to write words of truth. And he desired to put them together correctly. The NIV says it this way: "What he wrote was upright and true." Solomon connects the word with God. "Every use of the word reflects God's way of acting: the word reflects the fact that God's revelation comes to us through the word."[5]

In effect, Solomon pits God's Word against the ocean of words in our world. He sets God's Word against our word and affirms an ultimate reality and authority. We can find some nails of certainty to hang our perceptions of reality on. Absolutes do exist. There is propositional truth for humanity to know. It is God's Word—Scripture!

Jesus told His disciples, "If you abide in My word, then you are truly disciples of Mine; and you shall know the truth, and the truth shall make you free" (John 8:31, 32). The Word of God will be the only point of reality against the illusions and temptations of the last days. It is already true for our postmodern, relativistic day.

Hearing on Our Knees

I've been captivated recently by the preaching ministry of George Whitefield. During his lifetime many considered him the most brilliant and popular preacher the modern world has ever known. In the wake of his fearless preaching, revival swept across the British Isles, and the Great Awakening transformed the American colonies during the eighteenth century. When he died at the age of 55, Whitefield had preached 30,000 sermons at an average of 500 a year, 10 a week. Sometimes he preached 40 or more hours a week. People knew Whitefield for his humility and deep spirituality. One of the most incredible images he leaves to inspire us with is how to approach God's Word. How to read Scripture.

After his conversion Whitefield began to read the Bible through on his knees. For a time he laid aside all other books and devoted his study entirely to the Scriptures. "I got more true knowledge from reading the Book of God in one month, than I could *ever* have acquired from *all* the writings of men," he testified.[6] We can visualize him at 5:00 in the morning in his room over Harris's bookstore. He is on his knees with His Bible spread out before him. With intense concentration he reads. Finally he comes to his unique practice of "praying over every line and every word," feasting his mind and his heart upon it until its essential meaning has become a part of his very person.[7]

Reading Scripture on our knees. "Draw near to listen," Solomon

87

says (Eccl. 5:1). "God is in heaven and you are on earth; therefore let your words be few" (verse 2). "In many dreams and in many words there is emptiness. Rather, fear God" (verse 7).

We need to have a different attitude to God's Word, Solomon says. It is time we cease talking and let God speak. We must come to Scripture with a heart of worship, a heart that fears God and lets Him describe reality. Each of us must elevate God's Word to be the final word on all our moral and spiritual deliberations.

Here's how Ellen White puts it: "If men would but take the Bible as it reads, . . . a work would be accomplished that would make angels glad and that would bring into the fold of Christ thousands upon thousands who are now wandering in error. We should exert all the powers of the mind in the study of the Scriptures and should task the understanding to comprehend, as far as mortals can, the deep things of God; yet we must not forget that the docility and submission of a child is the true spirit of the learner. Scriptural difficulties can never be mastered by the same methods that are employed in grappling with philosophical problems. We should not engage in the study of the Bible with that self-reliance with which so many enter the domains of science, but with a prayerful dependence upon God and a sincere desire to learn His will. We must come with a humble and teachable spirit to obtain knowledge from the great I AM. Otherwise, evil angels will so blind our minds and harden our hearts that we shall not be impressed with the truth."[8]

James concurs: "In humility receive the word implanted, which is able to save your souls" (James 1:21). The implanted Word of God will never produce its intended purpose in our hearts and lives if we do not receive it with humility so that, as James goes on to say, we will be slow to anger (emotional resistance) and slow to speak (contradictory thoughts). In his book *The Great Divorce* C. S. Lewis writes: "There are only two kinds of people in the end: those who say to God, 'Thy will be done,' and those to whom God says, in the end, 'Thy will be done' "[9]

We are people of the Word, and yet we need a new attitude of obedience, a new attitude of listening. If we continue to bob in an ocean of words, will we be able to concentrate on our task, fulfill our mission?

---

[1] Walter Truett Anderson, *Reality Isn't What It Used to Be: Theatrical Politics, Ready-to-Wear Religion, Global Myths, Primitive Chic, and Other Wonders of the Postmodern World* (San Francisco: HarperSanFrancisco, 1990), p. ix.

[2] Timothy R. Phillips and Dennis Okholm, ed., *Christian Apologetics in the Postmodern World* (Downers Grove, Ill.: InterVarsity Press, 1995), p. 13.

[3] Anderson, p. 5.

[4] Roger Lundin, "The Pragmatics of Postmodernity," in *Christian Apologetics in the Postmodern World,* eds. Timothy R. Phillips and Dennis L. Okholm (Downers Grove, Ill.: InterVarsity Press, 1994), p. 30.

[5] J. Ellul, *Reason for Being,* p. 189.

[6] Ruth Gordon Short, *George Whitefield: Trumpet of the Lord* (Washington, D.C., Review and Herald Pub. Assn., 1979), p. 18.

[7] Arnold A. Dallimore, *George Whitefield: God's Anointed Servant in the Great Revival of the Eighteenth Century* (Westchester, Ill.: Crossway Books, 1990), p. 22.

[8] Ellen G. White, *The Great Controversy* (Mountain View, Calif.: Pacific Press Pub. Assn., 1950), p. 599.

[9] C. S. Lewis, *The Great Divorce* (New York: Macmillan Co., 1946), p. 69.

WAXEN WINGS AND THE NEANDERTHAL CHILD

Furthermore, I have seen under the sun that in the place of justice
there is wickedness, and in the place of righteousness there
is wickedness.
I said to myself, "God will judge both the righteous man and the
wicked man,"
for a time for every matter and for every deed is there.
I said to myself concerning the sons of men,
"God has surely tested them in order for them to see that they are
but beasts."
For the fate of the sons of men and the fate of beasts is the same.
As the one dies so dies the other;
indeed, they all have the same breath and there is
no advantage for man over beast, for all is vanity.
All go to the same place. All come from the dust and all return
to the dust.
Who knows that the breath of man ascends upward
and the breath of the beast descends downward to the earth?
And I have seen that nothing is better than that man should
be happy in his activities,
for that is his lot. For who will bring him to see what will
occur after him?
—Ecclesiastes 3:16-22

Daedalus and his son Icarus escaped from King Minos of Crete by flying over the Aegean Sea toward Sicily with artificial wings the father had made from wax and feathers. The father warned the son not to fly too high or the sun would melt the wax. But the boy, intoxicated with flight, soared above his cautious father. In the clear blue sky the warmth of the sun dissolved his delicate wings, causing him to plunge to his death in the green sea below.

The myth of Icarus is an old Greek tale that tells of how overweening human pride and vanity all too often bring tragedy. That's where Solomon brings us. "I said to myself concerning the sons of men, 'God has surely tested them in order for them to see that they are but beasts'" (Eccl. 3:18).

Why would God want us to see that we have nothing over the animal world? Because we are caught up with ourselves, that's why! We find ourselves trying to be all we can be, struggling to reach our fullest potential. Taking pride in our accomplishments, we are like Icarus, who was intoxicated with flight, exhilarated with the power to climb higher and higher. Our human family is drunk with itself and what it can be.

We catch a glimpse of that spirit in the tragic death of 7-year-old Jessica Dubroff. Jessica was going to be the youngest person to fly across the continent. Her Cessna had a booster seat so she could see through the windshield. Aluminum extenders helped her feet reach the floor pedals. Had Jessica completed her transcontinental air adventure, it would have been a spirit-lifting final story on the evening news. A tale of human triumph over which news anchors could smile winsomely and then say good night, leaving us with the feeling that all was right with the world, and that, yes, we humans have incredible potential to do or be whatever we set our minds to.[1]

We find it in the *Humanist Manifesto II* signed by hundreds of prominent philosophers, scientists, and intellectuals of every description. It declares that the twenty-first century should be the humanist century, the dawn of a new age. A century that will tap the creativity of each human being so that human progress and the values central to it will blossom. It will be a time in which we begin with humans, not God; nature, not deity. In it moral values will derive their source from human experience, thus making ethics autonomous and situational.[2]

Solomon knew about human pride and what it is like to be intoxicated with one's self, one's abilities. To be all we could be. That's the humanist's way to finding meaning in life. Begin with humans and refuse to accept any notion of human depravity and sinfulness. Assert your dignity and worth and potential. Invest life with meaning by the choices you make and the striving to be all you can be.

But God wants us to get a clearer picture of ourselves, of what we are really like when we live life *under the sun* in our own strength and without Him. Psalm 49:20 puts it this way: "Man who is in honor, yet does not understand, is like the beasts that perish" (NKJV). It is humanity in its pride and self-confidence that is in danger. Like Icarus, we are intoxicated with flight, and according to Solomon, we have waxen wings.

Just Another Animal?

When Solomon startles us by saying that no difference exists between human beings and beasts while we live without God *under the sun,* he sandwiches his thoughts between two anchor points, morality and mortality—evil and death.

"I have seen under the sun that in the place of justice there is wickedness, and in the place of righteousness there is wickedness" (Eccl. 3:16).

"I looked again at all the acts of oppression which were being done under the sun. And behold I saw the tears of the oppressed and that they had no one to comfort them; and on the side of their oppressors was power" (Eccl. 4:1).

In Ecclesiastes 4:3 Solomon refers to seeing "the evil activity that is done under the sun." It is hard for any one of us to miss the evil done in our world. Just look at Rwanda. "There are no devils left in hell. . . . They are all in Rwanda," Nancy Gibbs wrote in the after-math of the atrocities.[3] We could turn to the killing fields of the for-mer Yugoslavia or watch the Hezbollah and Israel slug it out.

Injustices, oppression, and evil activity reveal beastlike behavior. The evil we inflict on one another demonstrates the beastly charac-teristics of our nature and conduct. Sin eats away at our humanity so that the more we yield to it the more subhuman and brutelike we become. Our depravity knows no bounds. If you doubt that, take the time to look!

It's easy to say "That doesn't include me." Aleksandr Solzhen-itsyn felt that way until he got caught in Russia's human sewage dis-posal system. In *The Gulag Archipelago* he writes how pride grows in the human heart like lard on a pig, and how he personally came to understand that at the core he was no different than his KGB captors:

"If only it were all so simple! If only there were evil people some-where insidiously committing evil deeds, and it were necessary only to separate them from the rest of us and destroy them. But the line dividing good and evil cuts through the heart of every human being. And who is willing to destroy a piece of his own heart?

"During the life of any heart this line keeps changing place; sometimes it is squeezed one way by exuberant evil and sometimes it shifts to allow enough space for good to flourish. One and the same human being is, at various ages, under various circumstances, a totally different human being. At times he is close to being a devil, at times to sainthood. But his name doesn't change, and to that name we ascribe the whole lot, good and evil."[4]

I believe Solomon knew what he was talking about. His own ex-perience of sexual license, of following every passion and living on the level of the body and bodily sensations, made it clear to him that he was not that much different than animals. He challenges us to look within and examine the attitude of our own hearts, our imagi-nation, our words and actions. Consider, for example, the way we treat people.

Have you ever seen squashed frogs after a rainy night? We live in a rural area where a dirt road runs by our wooded lot and by several small ponds and lakes as well. When it pours down rain at night, the frogs just seem to come out of nowhere. As you drive along the road, your headlights show them hopping across the road. I have often walked this road after such a rain and been intrigued by all the squashed frogs I see along the way. By the next day they are already decomposing. If the weather is still moist, they turn into what looks like a jellied goo. Others are flatter than pancakes, and if a wind comes up soon after the rain, they are as dry as shoe leather, too. More than once I have asked myself as I passed those squashed creatures, "What is life? What difference is there between me and these unfortunate frogs?"

I saw a *Time* photo once that captured the terrible aftermath of flooding in Bangladesh. There, washed up together in a slowly receding pool, were the bloating bodies of humans and cattle. It was a grisly sight, human and animal bodies bobbing together in muddy waters. Same fate! Same end! I asked myself again, "What is life? What difference is there between animals and humans?"

Evidently Solomon saw the same types of things and asked the same questions! "For the fate of the sons of men and the fate of beasts is the same. As the one dies so dies the other; indeed, they all have the same breath. . . . All go to the same place. All came from the dust and all return to the dust" (Eccl. 3:19, 20). If you press Solomon's summation to the ultimate, do you know what he is saying? That the beast in the field today that dies and drops into a hole in the ground and turns back into dust has a future exactly like yours and mine. When we die, we get dropped into a hole and turn to dust. That's it. No advantage. Same fate, same death, same breath, same brevity, same origin, same destiny! We must ask ourselves, the text suggests, "What's the difference?" Without divine revelation no one would know what comes afterward. That is why cynicism, anxiety, spiritualism, and New Age speculations of all kinds fill our world. Death humbles our human pride, power, and idealism.

Solomon's language echoes Genesis 3. Part of God's purpose in the great controversy is to allow evil to run its course and to let death reign in the process. He does so in order to show that we, like animals, are equally a creation of God, equally subject to His will, and equally distant from Him. Death and the overflow of evil in our world and in our lives are to humble us before God.

Morality and mortality both press us with the questions: "What is the difference? Where is our glory? Where is our dignity? our identity? our advantage?" They force us to face the reality of life lived *under the sun* without God. We must lift our eyes *above the sun* for meaning and purpose, identity and dignity.

Crowned With Glory and Honor

In his book *Reality Isn't What It Used to Be* Walter Truett Anderson tells about a brochure he got in the mail once that offered the opportunity for him to get in touch with his primal instincts. *"A Spiritual Warrior's Journey.* With Tom Little Bear. $150.00. Join other men and women on a spiritual warrior's journey to reconnect with our primal instincts. Spend three days living the way our ancestors did for thousands of years, with the spirit of your power animal and the sacred mystical powers of the universe. You will learn how to make fire, arrows, lodges, all in the old way. Learn how to stalk, hunt, and gather your own food. We'll paint faces and dance, sing and drum together under the full moon. By building a sweat-lodge near a creek, we'll go through a series of purification ceremonies to cleanse our bodies, minds, and spirits of negatives and toxins and to come into a better relationship with the Great Spirit, our Mother Earth, and all things that surround us. This journey will forever change your life. Call for dates."[5]

People today think it's neat to go what Anderson calls "primitive chic." In his book *Dark Nature: A Natural History of Evil* Lyall Watson writes, "As a biologist I see no reason to exclude humans from my study. We are animals."[6]

"We like to see ourselves as something more than animals. As animal *plus*. The plus factor being some kind of special human essence that has been added to the baseline of animality,"[7] he says. Watson goes on to add that as a biologist he begins at the bottom and works up rather than at the top and work down.

Solomon takes the opposite point of view. Beginning at the top and working down, he tells us: "I found that though God has made men upright, each has turned away to follow his own downward road" (Eccl. 7:29, TLB). In other words, living on the level of the animal *under the sun* is to retrogress, degenerate, sink, fall back. That realization is hard to swallow for a world that refuses to accept the notion of human depravity and sinfulness. Humanity wants to begin with human beings and not God, making humanity the measure of humanity.

Ecclesiastes has a strong Creation theme. Solomon wrote it with the book of Genesis in hand.[8] "Remember also your Creator" (Eccl. 12:1), he tells us. No doubt he had the sixth day of Creation in mind: "Then God said, 'Let Us make man in Our image, according to Our likeness. . . . And God created man in His own image, in the image of God He created him; male and female He created them" (Gen. 1:26, 27), and God breathed into man the breath of life (Gen. 2:7).

Also he may have thought of the words of his father, David: "What is man, that Thou dost take thought of him? And the son of man, that Thou dost care for him? Yet Thou hast made him a little lower than God, and dost crown him with glory and majesty!" (Ps. 8:4, 5).

The image of God comprises a remarkable manifesto of human nature as described in Genesis. "The belief that we are created in God's image acknowledges that we humans are blessed with attributes that separate us from the purely instinct-driven creatures of the earth: free will, imagination, creativity, compassion, conscience, self-awareness, and a sense of the future."[9] The *imago dei* lays out three major principles on which our moral and spiritual life is predicated. *Identity:* our direct spiritual identity with God, who created us in His image. *Equality:* the fundamental equality and interdependence of the sexes. *Purpose:* preserving and replenishing God's creation.

As Naomi Rosenblatt says in her book *Wrestling With Angels:* "Being made in the image of God invests us with a portable spiritual center."[10] We can have an inner identity that accompanies us everywhere we go and can be a determining factor in every moral and spiritual situation we encounter.

Solomon confronts our modern age with the issue of creation/evolution. It is one of living *under the sun* or living *above the sun.* How we view Genesis is vital. Is it myth or history? Is it literal or idealized story? Are the days 24-hour periods or only imagery of larger spans of time? Our answers will determine whether our perspective reflects *under the sun* living or *above the sun* living. Whether we are but beasts—animals, as Lyall Watson says—or have dignity and identity rooted in the living God of heaven.

Ellen White tells us that Satan rejoices in his success in effacing the divine image from the minds of God's people.[11] Its restoration is part of our message to a dying world. The first angel's message presses it home to human hearts: "Fear God, and give Him glory, because the hour of His judgment has come; and worship Him who made the heaven and the earth and sea and springs of waters" (Rev. 14:7). The Sabbath is a crucial part of preserving this truth.

Our family was sitting around the table welcoming the Sabbath one Friday evening. We have a rather straightforward custom that doesn't really take that long, but is nevertheless meaningful to us. All of us simply sing "Welcome, Delightful Morn," a song that tells of our soaring from the low plains of mortal toys to reach immortal joy, and then we recite the fourth commandment. That's it! It's about all four boys really want or need. On this night, though, I lingered a bit. I shared with them a recent publication by an evangelical Christian who was pushing the notion of theistic evolution. His point was rather simple. In a nutshell he said that evangelical Christians who believe Genesis 1 and 2 as seven literal 24-hour days have bought into Seventh-day Adventist hermeneutics. He was essentially arguing, If you don't want to be branded with the Adventists, you need to accept theistic evolution.

Then I shared some things that I had learned about a favorite author of mine, John R. Stott. Stott has written an incredible spiritually moving and powerful book on substitutionary atonement titled *The Cross of Christ*. And yet he too believes in theistic evolution. I could not help wondering out loud to my sons if his views on the nature and origin of humanity undercut his position on substitutionary atonement and our need of a Saviour. Of course it does.

Like Icarus we're soaring high in our own thoughts and our own potential. But as Solomon says, we have waxen wings. Life lived *under the sun* brings us down to the level of the animal. Such a moral crash leaves us with no more dignity or hope than a squashed frog in the road. Ellen White reminds us that "Christ came that He might recreate the image of God in man."[12] I believe that's Solomon's point. Our waxen wings have melted. Our thinking has blurred to the place that we assume we're Neanderthal children, still on our way up.

During the fourth century a monk named Telemachus spent most of his life in a remote community of prayer, raising vegetables for the cloister kitchen. When he was not tending his garden spot, he was happily fulfilling his vocation of study and prayer. Then one day he felt the Lord leading him to go to Rome, the political center of his world. Telemachus wondered why God was drawing him to Rome. He didn't fit a bustling wealthy city. Instead, he felt more comfortable in his quiet little cloistered community, a sheltered spiritual garden where his convictions were deepening and his faith in God was strong. But he couldn't fight God's direction. So he left.

By and by he reached the busy streets of Rome, and what he saw stunned him. The people were angry and preoccupied. On one occasion the bewildered monk found himself swept up by a crowd. Finally he wound up in a place he didn't even know existed: the Colosseum, where animalistic gladiators fought and killed one another for little reason other than the amusement of the thousands that gathered in Rome's public stadium.

He stared in disbelief as one gladiator after another stood be-

fore the emperor and said, "We who are about to die salute thee."
He put his hands to his ears when he heard the clashing swords
and shields, as one man after another fought to his death. Finally
he couldn't stand it any longer. But what in the world could he do?
He was nothing! Still, he jumped up on top of the perimeter wall
and cried, "In the name of Christ, forbear!" He could not endure
such senseless killing. "Stop this now!" No one listened. They kept
applauding the fight as it went on. Another man fell. Finally, unable to contain himself, he leaped down onto the sandy floor of the
arena. What a comic figure he must have appeared to be—of slight
build, a small man in a monk's habit, dashing back and forth between muscular, brutal fighters. Again he shouted, "In the name of
Christ, forbear!"

The crowd looked at him and sneered, and one of the gladiators,
with his shield, bumped him aside and went after his opponent.
Finally Telemachus became an irritation to the crowd as well as the
gladiators. Some in the stand yelled, "Run him through! Kill him!"
The same gladiator that had pushed him aside with his shield came
down against his chest and opened his stomach with one flash of the
sword. As he slumped to his knees, the little monk gasped once
more, "In the name of Christ . . . forbear!"

Then a strange thing occurred. As the two gladiators and the
crowd focused on the still form on the suddenly crimson sand, the
arena grew deathly quiet. Then someone in the top tier got up and
walked out. Another followed. All over the arena spectators began to
leave, until the huge stadium stood empty. There were other forces
at work, of course, but that innocent figure lying in the pool of blood
crystallized the opposition to the public games, and that was the last
gladiatorial contest in the Roman Colosseum.

When we live for ourselves *under the sun,* with self and humanity
our only measure of identity and purpose as we strive to be all we
can be, we regress, sink, morally crash. But if we've been gripped
with our heritage as children of God redeemed by Jesus Christ, who
is restoring the image of God within, we will be different.

―――――

[1] "Jessica's Final Flight," *Newsweek,* Apr. 22, 1996, pp. 25-27; "Fly Till I Die," *Time,* Apr. 22, 1996, pp. 35-38.

[2] Burton F. Porter, *Reason for Living: A Basic Ethics* (New York: MacMillan Pub. Co., 1988), pp. 346-352.

[3] Nancy Gibbs, in *Time,* May 16, 1994, p. 57.

[4] Aleksandr Solzhenitsyn, *The Gulag Archipelago* (New York: Harper & Row, 1973), vol. 1, p. 168.

[5] W. T. Anderson, *Reality Isn't What It Used to Be,* p. 193.

[6] Lyall Watson, *Dark Nature: A Natural History of Evil* (New York: Harper Collins, 1995), p. 104.

[7] *Ibid.,* p. xiii.

[8] W. C. Kaiser, *Ecclesiastes: Total Life,* pp. 36, 37.

[9] Naomi H. Rosenblatt, *Wrestling With Angels: What the First Family of Genesis Teaches Us About Our Spiritual Identity, Sexuality, and Personal Relationships* (New York: Delacorte Press, 1995), p. xix.

[10] *Ibid.,* pp. 14, 15.

[11] White, *Fundamentals of Christian Education* (Nashville: Southern Pub. Assn., 1923), p. 499.

[12] ―――――, *The Desire of Ages* (Mountain View, Calif.: Pacific Press Pub. Assn., 1898), p. 478.

10

MY FAIR LADY

"Behold I have discovered this,"
says the Preacher,
"Adding one thing to another to find an explanation,
which I am still seeking but have not found.
I have found one man among a thousand,
but I have not found a woman among all these.
Behold, I have found only this,
that God made men upright,
but they have sought out many devices."
—Ecclesiastes 7:27-29

Which translation of Ecclesiastes 7:28 do you prefer?

"One man among a thousand I have found, but a woman among all these I have not found" (NKJV).

"I found only one man in a thousand who was good and could be trusted, but such women were even harder to find" (Clear Word).

"I found one upright man among a thousand, but not one upright woman among them all" (NIV).

"One tenth of one percent of the men I interviewed could be said to be wise, but not one woman!" (TLB).

"One man in a thousand I may find, but never a woman better than the rest" (Jerusalem).

"I found one man in a thousand that I could respect, but not one woman" (TEV).

Whichever one you choose, it raises some difficult questions. Was Solomon a male chauvinist pig? Did he look at women only from the neck down? One wonders, because of his harem of 700 wives and 300 concubines and this pithy little statement. Is it an example of ancient Middle Eastern culture coming through in Scripture? Something that needs to be stripped away or reapplied? I mean, it can't be true, can it?

No doubt some men read this passage with glee and run with it to excuse their female bashing and exert male dominance. Others see it as just one more proof that Scripture is out of touch culturally and shouldn't be taken literally. Still others will try to interpret it in a way that isn't so harsh, so that it doesn't say what it seems to advocate.

What is Solomon saying, anyway?

Having thought long and hard on this one, I knew I couldn't avoid it as a subject in this book. But in the process I've felt like Solomon, who asked, "Who is like a wise man and who knows the interpretation of a matter?" (Eccl. 8:1). In her book *Ten Stupid Things Women Do to Mess Up Their Lives,* Laura Schlessinger writes: "This book is going to be difficult for you to read—and maybe even hurtful to you—and you may get angry. There are ten million exceptions to everything I say. Nonetheless, EVERYTHING I SAY IS TRUE!"[1] That's how I feel about some of the things I am about to share. They are candid straight shots without any holds barred. It may be difficult for some of us to face them. Ten million exceptions exist for everything I might say. Nonetheless, *everything I say is true!*

First, I want to affirm that what Solomon writes is inspired. I refuse to accept what I have found many scholars arguing: that Ecclesiastes is filled with heresies, half-truths, and cynicism. That it is the words of a confused man who barely gets a grip on life in the final chapter. Rather, I accept Ellen White's view that Solomon was writing at a time of his life when he did have his act together. In fact, God inspired him to share his spiritual journey and to show where the real issues of life lie. I find Ecclesiastes very candid, but solid and trustworthy in its message. There is no getting around what Solomon said here. Our challenge is understanding what he said and why.

Second, I want to affirm that by the time he wrote these words, Solomon held a very high view of women. He knew and wrote about the virtuous woman whose life left a sweet essence of spiritual influence and moral power. The kind of woman that men would speak about with respect and awe at the city gates (Prov. 31:10-31). Furthermore, Solomon personified "wisdom" as a woman (Prov. 9:1-6; 1:20, 21; 8:1-36; 2:2-4). This is no mere literary device. Solomon wrote with Genesis in mind. He knew the story of Adam— alone in the garden, incomplete, vulnerable, unable to make it on his own. God gave him Eve as a helper. She was the crowning moment of Creation because she would make Adam complete and enable him to live life fully and responsibly. So with "wisdom." Humanity's a fool without wisdom, being vulnerable and unable to make it in life. We need her—wisdom! Solomon actually presents an extremely high view of woman and a unique understanding of Genesis!

So what is Solomon saying in our passage? Let me make one more point before I answer. Whatever Solomon implies in Ecclesiastes 7:28, he says more clearly in the next verse. Verse 29 is the key! "I found that though God has made men upright, each has turned away to follow his own downward road" (TLB). Solomon was searching for a man who would have his act together and fulfill God's ideal. He sought a woman who had her act together and fulfilled God's ideal. But each—male and female—had turned to follow his or her own downward road.

Here's how I read verse 28: "When I was with men and trying to work through some of these answers, I found one in a thousand." That's another way of saying that it was very, very rare.

Now here's what I think Solomon said next: "But I found I couldn't discover it when I worked to perceive it with the women of my life."[2]

Solomon turned to the sphere of human relationships in his

search for wisdom. In doing so he exposes us to the part that sin can play on both sides of an encounter between the sexes. Verse 26 refers to a deeply disillusioning entanglement with a "woman whose heart is snares and nets, whose hands are chains." That kind of experience with a woman can jade you. It can distort, even destroy, any subsequent attempt at meaningful relationships. Solomon no doubt escaped this particular woman's grip, but did not leave undamaged. His fruitless search for a woman he could trust tells us as much about himself and his approach to female relationships as it does about any of his female acquaintances.[3]

I believe Solomon candidly reveals himself here as being dysfunctional when it comes to women. And he depicts how women, too, can be dysfunctional when it involves relationships with men. He admits to an unhealthy interaction. In doing so, Solomon plunges us headlong into the gender debate and the vision God has for every one of us—male and female. Solomon is talking about what God made us to be in His image and with each other, and what we have become instead.

My Fair Lady?

One of my wife's favorite videos is *My Fair Lady*. Remember Henry Higgins exclaiming, "Why can't a woman be more like a man?" It is a tale about male attitudes toward women, of how they see and treat them. The movie depicts how selfish and bigoted and insensitive and controlling men can be, how they come to women with their own agenda, their own needs, and often their out-of-control passions. I've already suggested that Solomon's fruitless search for a woman he could trust may tell us as much about himself and his approach to women as about any of the women in his life. There was a time in his life when Solomon looked at women merely from the neck down. For what he could get out of the relationship. He used women to fill his physical and emotional needs and thus found himself in one trap after another. Eventually he would say: "When it came to the women in my life, I couldn't find one who had it together enough to make any difference" (Eccl. 7:28, my paraphrase).

For the most part, men in our culture have unhealthy attitudes toward women. We're no different from Henry Higgins or Solomon. A pastor long enough to get a good look at what women put up with, I could tell lots of stories about husbands and live-ins who have brought an incredible amount of pain to the women in their lives. Susan Forward has written a book she titled *Men Who Hate Women and the Women Who Love Them*. Just the title says volumes. *The Silence of Adam* is Larry Crabb's exposé of male abdication of moral and spiritual responsibility in the home and marriage. Men cause a lot of pain and anguish in our homes and marriages. There are a lot of plain old bigoted men out there. Our attitudes find expression in a host of ways: controlling behavior, sexual harassment, keeping the checkbook to ourselves, abuse (sexual, physical, verbal, psychological), and irresponsibility. A *Time* article tells how more than at any other time in the past 25 years men are living in a state of radical disconnection from women and children.[4]

Twice now our Adventist family (especially the North American Division) has engaged the question of the ordination of women to the gospel ministry. It has been a wrenching experience for many, but a growing one as well. No matter how the church decides on the biblical, theological, and ecclesiological aspects of this sensitive issue, there is one thing that absolutely needs to change—male attitudes about women! It is the moral side of the equation. I have been intrigued to observe how some of our Adventist male leaders (and others) at times would publicly opt for a politically correct position on women's ordination, but in their private lives continue some very bigoted male behavior toward both the women in their lives and women in general. I've observed the same too among Adventist men who do not feel women's ordination appropriate. But I had better quit before I get myself in trouble!

Ten Stupid Things

In her book *Ten Stupid Things Women Do to Mess Up Their Lives,* Laura Schlessinger, a popular, often controversial psychotherapist who hosts a nationally syndicated, top-rated midday radio talk show, brings an interesting twist to the gender debate. "The current feminist agenda," she writes, "mostly accuses men or society in general, thereby ignoring the pivotal role played by women themselves in their life predicaments."[5] She presses women to take a good hard look at their attitudes, behaviors, and decisions, and to realize that they not only mess up their own lives, but the lives of others as well.

That's where Solomon brings us in verse 26—to a "woman whose heart is snares and nets." To a woman "whose hands are chains." According to Genesis, woman was to impart strength and bring man to his highest point and his completion. Woman was the height of Creation and should epitomize everything good, beautiful, and wise. But here she becomes, instead, a trap that crushes and bruises man. What is Solomon saying? When a woman replaces love with seduction, manipulation, and the shackles of sexuality, she is more bitter than death. The height of Creation, the one to epitomize everything good, beautiful, and wise, she becomes the depth of failure, representing everything that is destructive. Yes, Solomon was looking at women from the neck down, but the women in his life knew how to play the game. They could twist him and maneuver him emotionally and spiritually. As 1 Kings 11 tells us, the women in his life turned him away from God: "When Solomon was old, his wives turned his heart away after other gods; and his heart was not wholly devoted to the Lord his God" (verse 4). It makes me think of men I know who have written God off or never joined the church because of the women in their lives—even so-called Christian women! Tragically, Adventist women as well.

Solomon will tell us in Proverbs: "The wise woman builds her house, but the foolish tears it down with her own hands" (Prov.

14:1). He will also say: "It is better to live in a corner of a roof, than in a house shared with a contentious woman" (Prov. 21:9). "It is better to live in a desert land, than with a contentious and vexing woman" (verse 19). "A constant dripping on a day of steady rain and a contentious woman are alike" (Prov. 27:15). He will also speak of the seductive, manipulative woman.

My wife and I became friends with a conservative evangelical couple whose earnestness and commitment to Christ is inspiring. The wife, Terry, told my wife that she and her husband had been going round and round over his interest in cigars. Finally she put her foot down and said, "Not in my house, you won't!" That was it. But one night, while praying about being a better wife, Terry heard an inner voice saying, "Let Paul smoke cigars if he wants to." The thought made her burst into tears, but she decided to follow what she considered God's promptings. When she informed Paul that he could smoke cigars in the house if he wanted to, he responded by saying he would do it just in the closed mud room off the kitchen.

"No," she said, "you can smoke in your favorite chair in the living room if you wish." Her point to Kathie was that "Paul hasn't smoked many cigars, but it sure changed our relationship with each other. It was a tangible moment of releasing my controlling tendencies and letting Paul work through his own Christian experience!"

Schlessinger's list of stupid things is pretty candid.[6] Things such as using marriage as a quick fix for low or no self-esteem. Or making babies for the wrong reason—as a jump start for love, personal growth, and commitment. Having sex too soon, thus setting oneself up to get burned. Living with a guy in hopes he'll want you! Putting up with abuse, control, and subjugation. Whining and whimpering. Carrying the blame. And when he's adulterous, addicted, controlling, insensitive, or violent—just hanging on in codependence.

Common Grace

Have you ever reached up and done a high five with someone?

It takes some coordination, doesn't it? Britty and Abby do it all the time. The two hands that meet in a high five, though, are attached to one body. Brittany and Abigail are the Hensel twins, conjoined for life. Their story is both a medical mystery and a lesson in cooperation for us all. They have two heads but share a single two-legged body. Two people above the waist with separate heads and necks, separate hearts, stomachs, and spinal cords, they become one below, having a common body.

Abigail controls the right hand and leg, Brittany the left. Their nervous systems are distinct. Tickle Abby on her side anywhere from head to toe, and Britty can't feel it. The girls experience separate hungers, separate urges to urinate and sleep, separate tastes. But they've learned how to do high fives, walk, ride a bike, swim. Through a miracle of determination, encouragement, and teamwork their separate brains and personalities have become synchronized to accomplish complex motions and goals. Theirs is a most intimate bond, sharing a more profound and intimate nature than most of us can imagine. They demonstrate the real meaning of individuality and the limitless power of human cooperation.[7]

God split His likeness into two halves. It takes both genders to reflect His image. For His image to be realized in us, we need to be what He has made us to be—male and female, both individually and in relationship to one another.

I believe the subtle flip side of Solomon's story of dysfunction and being hurt and disappointed by the women in his life is the question of his being there to build women up so they could be what God had intended them to be. I can hear him asking himself, after sowing all those wild oats, "What kind of atmosphere have I created for the development and growth of her potential? What climate have I established for her or someone else to bloom?"

Stan Thornburg tells us what that means in an article he wrote called "On Becoming a Safe Male."[8] For the most part, he notes, men in our culture are not safe for women. He asks, "Where are the men to whom women can relate in absolute safety? Where are the men who don't, in their thoughts, body language, preferences, or humor, objectify and degrade women?" The "safe male," he says, assigns worth to a woman because she shares God's image, not because of her body shape, color of hair, personality, or talents. He keeps his ego in check and takes responsibility for his sexual responses. Listening to women, he seeks to empower them and encourage them in positive, tangible ways. Such men have purity and integrity so that a woman can feel free to approach them without fear or intimidation.

The focus of Promise Keepers includes male attitudes toward women. "The Seven Promises of a Promise Keeper" include honoring Jesus through worship; prayer and obedience to Bible teachings; commitment to practicing spiritual, moral, and sexual purity; the commitment to building strong marriages and families through love, protection, and biblical values; influencing the world; and being obedient to Christ.[9]

But the same is true for women. What kind of atmosphere are they creating for the development and growth potential of the men in their lives? What climate are they establishing for their sons, husbands, work associates, or someone else to bloom? Proverbs 31 points the way. It tells of a virtuous woman whose life leaves a sweet essence of spiritual influence and moral power—the kind of woman men speak about with respect and awe at the city gates.

God has given woman a tremendous capacity to influence others. Her communication skills, her focus on deep relationships and care for others, and the physical attractiveness designed by God are all ways women influence. The Hebrew word "helper" is *azer,* which means to "surround." When women surround the men and women in their life with their relational skills and their care for others they become women of impact.[10]

Abigail's influence on David is a biblical classic. David was all charged up with anger and out to take revenge for the ill treatment he received from Abigail's husband Nabal. But Abigail came to him with the right words said in the right way as well as being gifted with a beautiful female body. And David goes away, not saying, "Wow, what a woman," but praising God. It's an incredible image of communication skill, beauty, and sensitivity that influences a man to honor God.

Psychologist Theodor Reik has a perceptive analysis: "In our civilization men are afraid that they will not be men enough, and women are afraid that they might be considered only women."[11] In the Hollywood comedy *Tootsie* (in which an out-of-work fellow disguises himself as a woman so he can land a job) Dustin Hoffman finds himself saying to a woman at work he has come to love: "I was a better man to you as a woman than I ever was to a woman as a man, if you see what I mean. Now I've got to learn to do it without a skirt on."

It takes some jarring of our minds sometimes. A friend of mine tells of working in a secular male environment. Day after day she put up with catcalls, lewd remarks, unfair workloads, and pornography. There in the staff locker room were the latest pinups pasted inside doors for all to see when swung open. She complained, but to no avail. Well, my friend, not a Christian at the time, had some grit. She bought a few copies of *Playgirl* and proceeded to hang up some really lurid pictures of men on her locker. Guess what? The men, disgusted, wanted her to take them down, and complained to the boss. Finally her boss ruled there would be no more pornography at all. She had made her point. Things changed as her work environment became more sensitive to the presence and feelings of women.

We have to get a grip on what we think about and how we relate to each other as male and female. Solomon, in raising the question of relationships, opens the way to issues of role and function. Whatever role we find ourselves in, though, God wants us to be the best man or the best woman we can be. Only in the context of being the best man and the best woman—and being open to where the other gender is and how they might feel—will the issue of gender roles in the context of Bible teaching become more clear.

Solomon said: "I found only one man in a thousand, but no

women." If a woman were writing Ecclesiastes, she'd no doubt have penned, "I have found only one woman in a thousand, but I haven't found any men." We're both in need of grace—male and female! As it says in verse 29, God made us upright, but we all have gone—male and female—down our own way. We have not been choosing or behaving correctly. Our attitudes need adjusting. Today the Holy Spirit of God says to our hearts—whether we are male or female—that it is time to confess our sins. It is time to acknowledge our attitudes, behavior, and manipulation. Whatever it is that needs changing in our male/female relationships, it is time to lay ourselves at the feet of Jesus and seek His restoring power so that we can become all He has created us to be. So we can become all He has died for us to be. And in so doing, through our male/female relationships, we will give our watching world a powerful new look at what it means to be made in God's image.

[1] Laura Schlessinger, *Ten Stupid Things Women Do to Mess Up Their Lives* (New York: HarperPerennial, 1994), p. xv.

[2] C. Swindoll, *Living on the Ragged Edge*, p. 216.

[3] D. Kidner, *The Message of Ecclesiastes*, p. 72.

[4] Barbara Ehrenreich, "Whose Gap Is It, Anyway?" *Time*, May 6, 1996, p. 36.

[5] Schlessinger, p. 225.

[6] *Ibid.*, pp. xiii, xiv.

[7] Claudia Wallis, "The Most Intimate Bond," *Time*, Mar. 25, 1966, pp. 60-64.

[8] Stan Thornburg, "On Becoming a Safe Male," *Discipleship Journal* 77 (September/October 1993): 65-67.

[9] *Seven Promises of a Promise Keeper* (Colorado Springs, Colo.: Focus on the Family Publishing, 1994).

[10] Vollie Sanders, "Biblical Femininity: What Does It Mean to Be a Woman?" *Discipleship* 77 (September/October 1993): 52-55.

[11] As quoted in N. H. Rosenblatt, *Wrestling With Angels*, p. 23.

FLOATING LAWN CHAIRS AND THE HAPPY MEDIUM

Do not be excessively righteous,
and do not be overly wise.
Why should you ruin yourself?
Do not be excessively wicked,
and do not be a fool.
Why should you die before your time?
It is good that you grasp the one thing,
and also not let go of the other;
for the one who fears God
comes forth with both of them.

—*Ecclesiastes 7:16-18*

L arry Walters was a truck driver, but his lifelong dream was to fly. When he graduated from high school, he joined the Air Force in hopes of becoming a pilot. Unfortunately, though, poor eyesight disqualified him. So when he finally left the service, he had to satisfy himself with watching others fly the fighter jets that crisscrossed the skies over his backyard. As he sat there in his lawn chair, he dreamed about the magic of flying.

Then one day Larry got an idea. He went down to the local Army-Navy surplus store and bought a tank of helium and 45 weather balloons. Not your average brightly colored party balloons, they were heavy-duty balloons measuring more than four feet across when fully inflated. Back in his yard, Larry used straps to attach the balloons to his lawn chair. He anchored the chair to the bumper of his jeep and inflated the balloons with helium. Then he packed some sandwiches and drinks and loaded a BB gun, figuring he could pop a few of those balloons when it was time to come back down.

His preparations complete, Larry Walters sat in his chair and cut the anchoring cord. His plan was to lazily float up a ways and lazily float back down. But things didn't quite work out that way. When he cut the cord, he didn't float lazily up—he shot up as if fired from a cannon! Nor did he go up a couple hundred feet. He climbed and climbed until he leveled off at 11,000 feet! At that height, he could hardly risk deflating any of the balloons, lest he unbalance the load and really experience flying. So he stayed up there, sailing around for 14 hours, totally at a loss as to how to get down.

Eventually Larry drifted into the approach corridor for Los Angeles International Airport. A Pan Am pilot radioed the tower about passing a guy in a lawn chair at 11,000 feet with a gun in his lap. LAX is right on the ocean, and the winds on the coast begin to change at nightfall. So as dusk fell, Larry began drifting out to sea. At that point the Navy dispatched a helicopter to rescue him. But the rescue team had a hard time getting to him, because the draft from their propeller kept pushing his homemade contraption away. Eventually they were able to hover over him and drop a rescue line to haul him in gradually.

As soon as Larry hit the ground, the authorities arrested him. But as they led him away in handcuffs, a television reporter called out, "Mr. Walters, why'd you do it?" Larry stopped, eyed the guy, then replied nonchalantly, "A man can't just sit around."[1]

We might think Larry Walters took his passion for flying a little too far. That his flying lawn chair was recklessly foolish. But for Larry, it sure beat just sitting around.

Some of us might think that Solomon is asking us to "just sit around" morally or spiritually—"Do not be excessively righteous. . . .

Do not be excessively wicked. . . . It is good that you grasp one thing, and also not let go of the other" (Eccl. 7:16-18). In other words, don't be too holy, and don't be too great a sinner, either. Find the happy medium. Play it safe!

That kind of thinking fits into our modern secular world. Some contemporary Adventists also have bought into that kind of thinking. Without doubt Solomon is talking about avoiding extremes and finding balance in our lives. But is he counseling us to just sit around lukewarm without spiritual passion? Is he saying it's all right to sin in moderation? Is he calling us to be a little earthly as well as a little heavenly? To have one foot propped nicely in both?

The Happy Medium

The April 1995 *Arizona Republic* reported how Steve Tran tried to rid his Westminster, California, apartment of cockroaches. Steve set off 25 bug bombs. When he closed the door to his apartment, he thought he had seen the last of the cockroaches that shared it with him. But when the spray reached the pilot light of the stove, it ignited, blasting his doors across the street, breaking all his windows, and setting his furniture on fire. "I really wanted to kill all of them," he said. "I thought if I used a lot more, it would last longer." According to the label, just two canisters of the fumigant would have solved Steve's problem. The blast produced more than $10,000 damage to his apartment building. And the cockroaches? "Well," Steve reported, "by Sunday, I saw them walking around again."[2]

There's danger in "overdoing it," Solomon writes. Like Steve Tran, our human nature tends to extremes. Setting off too many bug bombs, we walk out the door thinking we have our problems solved, but in the end we only create more problems, and the original need in our life still exists.

If we're too "goody-goody," Solomon says, we'll ruin ourselves. He's talking about how we can become foolishly fanatical and model an out-of-balance Christianity. Straining at externals, we find ourselves trapped in legalism. Although doing more for the Lord, we enjoy it less. Through our habits and priorities and religious eccentricities we can cut ourselves off from family and friends and simply not relate to real life. When we overdo, we become a laughingstock, our religion becomes empty, and our spiritual assurance vanishes.

On the other hand, if we go off the deep end in sin, we're fools, and there's a good chance we'll shorten our life. Solomon's talking about how we can react to legalism and spiritual extremism by letting the pendulum swing the other way toward doing what we think is OK—an approach that most of the time leads more and more toward what our own human nature wants to do. It can easily get out of hand until we become extremists, such as Dennis Rodman, the radical tattoo-covered Chicago Bulls player who likes to butt heads and chase hot women. He stripped down to his tattoos for the jacket of his new book, *Bad as I Wanna Be*.[3] That's the subtle flip side to spiritual extremism—being as good or bad as we want to be.

Verse 18 captures Solomon's point: "It is good that you grasp one thing, and also not let go of the other." In other words, hang on to what he says in verse 16 with one hand—"Don't be too good or too wise!" (TLB)—while not letting go with the other hand of what he cautions in verse 17: "Don't be too wicked either—don't be a fool!" (TLB). Balance is the key! But does this mean that a little sin is all right? Can we sin with moderation? Can we, like Dennis Rodman, decide to be as bad as we want to be or as good as we want to be as long as we keep balanced? Does it mean that we should never be conscientious or passionate about the specific things God has told us in His Word or the writings of Ellen G. White?

Solomon is not advising us to obey God halfheartedly or sin against Him periodically. Rather, he wants us to be spiritually mature, spiritually perceptive. He longs for us to have the ability to see clearly the dangers of both extremes and walk the straight and narrow path between them. The ancient king has in mind the insight to determine the difference between fanatical extremism and careful obedience. The ability to remain steadfast in a time when a secular world may consider our faith radical and unreasonable. Each of us must learn to cut through the contemporary fog of all those supposed "gray" areas in which people say "It really doesn't make a difference" or "These are peripheral issues" or "It's a cultural thing" or "Be whatever you wanna be as long as you're sincere." Solomon calls for us to balance conscientious outward obedience to the specific commands of God's Word with an inner-heart understanding of the principles those concrete commands express.

Vertical Coffins or a Place to Dance?

Late one morning in 1984 Dr. Charles Garfield drove through a toll-booth on his way to lunch in San Francisco. He had passed tollbooths at the Oakland-San Francisco Bay Bridge thousands of times and never had an exchange worth remembering with anybody. A relationship with a person in a tollbooth is one of those "nonencounters" of life. You hand over some money; you might get some change; you drive off. But on this morning Garfield heard loud music. It sounded like a party, or a Michael Jackson concert. He looked around but saw no other cars with their windows open or sound trucks parked nearby. Glancing at the tollbooth, he saw the man inside dancing. "What are you doing?" Garfield asked.

"I'm having a party," the attendant replied.

"What about the rest?" Garfield asked as he looked over at the other booths and saw the people in them just sitting with apparent boredom.

"They're not invited," the guy replied. Garfield had a dozen other questions, but someone behind him started blowing the horn, so he paid his fare and drove off. But he made a mental note to himself to find the guy again. *Something in his eyes says there's magic in his tollbooth,* he thought.

Months later he did encounter the attendant again, still with the loud music. "What are you doing?" Garfield asked.

"Hey, I remember you from the last time," the man answered. "I'm still dancing. I'm having the same party."

116

"Look," Garfield said, "what about the rest of the people—"

"Stop," the man replied. Then pointing down the row of toll-booths, he asked, "What do those look like to you?"

"They look like . . . tollbooths."

"Noooooooo imagination!" the attendant sneered.

"OK, I give up. What do they look like to you?"

"Vertical coffins!" he exclaimed.

"What are you talking about?" Garfield persisted.

"I can prove it. At 8:30 every morning live people get in. They die for eight hours. At 4:30, like Lazarus from the dead, they reemerge and go home. For eight hours their brains are on hold, dead on the job. Going through the motions."

"Why is it different for you?" Garfield questioned.

The man looked at him and said, "I'm going to be a dancer someday." Then pointing to the administration building, he added, "My bosses are in there, and they're paying for my training."

Driving away, Garfield thought to himself, *Sixteen people dead on the job, and the seventeenth, in precisely the same situation, figures out a way to live. He's having a party where most of us would proba-bly not last three days.* Later Garfield asked the guy out for lunch, during which he said, "I don't understand why anybody would think my job is boring. I have a corner office, glass on all sides. I can see the Golden Gate, San Francisco, the Berkeley hills. Half the Western world vacations here . . . and I just stroll in every day and practice dancing."[4]

Most of us are in "vertical coffins"! We're neither too holy nor too bad, but somewhere in the middle. Revelation calls it lukewarm: not hot, not cold, just "kind of there." But that's not the type of bal-ance Solomon is talking about here. He's calling us to live for God in the midst of the extremes we're so prone toward. He wants us to live for God in the midst of the extremes we seek to avoid—and to live for God with a passion! With music in your ears and a dance in your life, find your way between the extremes. Don't stand all day long in a vertical coffin, putting your spiritual/moral brain on hold.

"Get some excitement in your life," Solomon says; "fear God." "The one who fears God" has it together (verse 18).

Solomon has in mind a passion for God that compels us to be and to do things not out of excess, not out of extremism, but out of love for God. When we fear God, we won't buy into contemporary secular mediocrity. Nor will we be lackadaisical about sin or pharisaically pursue righteousness as an end in itself. Instead, our heart will be on fire with a passion for Him that will bring biblical balance into our lives. Fearing God will produce radical obedience, radical lifestyle, and radical witness—but never extremism or fanaticism. Obedient, committed disciples are not "goody-goodies."

Oswald Chambers, who wrote the classic devotional *My Utmost for His Highest* (first published in 1935 and recently ranked third among nonfiction Christian best-selling titles) wrote: "The surest sign that God has done a work of grace in my heart is that I love Jesus Christ best; not weakly and faintly, not intellectually, but passionately, personally and devotedly, overwhelming every other love of my life."[5]

That's the spiritual passion God's end-time people will have! And that's what our final generation needs to see! It is a passion for Jesus, for truth, obedience, and for righteousness, but it's a passion that's in balance, that commends itself to the intelligent mind of a watching searching world.

---

[1] Howard Hendricks, *Standing Together* (Gresham, Oreg.: Vision House Publishing, Inc., 1995), pp. 121-123; Cecil Adams, *Return of the Straight Dope* (New York: Ballantine Books, 1994), pp. 131, 132.

[2] *Leadership,* Spring 1996, p. 68.

[3] "A Wild Bull Bares All," *Newsweek,* May 13, 1996, p. 81.

[4] Charles Garfield, "A Place to Stand," in Jack Canfield and Mark Victor Hansen, eds., *A Second Helping of Chicken Soup for the Soul* (Dearfield Beach, Fla.: Health Communications, 1995), pp. 175-177.

[5] As quoted in E. Young, *The Meaning of Life,* p. 225.

HAVE A BLAST
WHILE YOU LAST?

For whoever is joined with the living,

  there is hope;

  surely a live dog is better than a dead lion.

For the living know they will die;

  but the dead do not know anything,

  nor have they any longer a reward,

  for their memory is forgotten.

Indeed their love, their hate, and their zeal have already perished,

  and they will no longer have a share in all that is done

  under the sun.

Go then,

  eat your bread in happiness, and drink your wine with

  a cheerful heart;

  for God has already approved your works.

Let your clothes be white all the time,

  and let not oil be lacking on your head.

Enjoy life with the woman whom you love

  all the days of your fleeting life which He has given to

  you under the sun;

  for this is your reward in life, and in your toil in which

  you have labored under the sun.

Whatever your hand finds to do,

  verily, do it with all your might;

for there is no activity or planning or wisdom in Sheol where you are going.

—Ecclesiastes 9:4-10

In May 1996, 31 climbers from five expeditions reached the almost-six-mile-high rock- and ice-covered summit of Mount Everest. But as they stood there at the top of the world, they noticed ominous clouds approaching from the valley below. Within hours a monstrous storm with shrieking winds blew horizontal sheets of snow at 65 knots. Visibility dropped to zero. The windchill plunged to –140°F. By the next day eight were dead. Some who survived came back with hands so frozen they clinked like glasses, and dead black flesh peeled from their faces. Two were emergency airlifted off the mountain.

One who didn't make it was Rob Hall, chief guide of the New Zealand expedition. He stopped to help an ailing American, and that's as far as he got. The brutal storm made his escape impossible. Two rescuers came within 200 yards of reaching him, but the pounding winds beat them back. When Hall learned over his radiophone that they would not be able to help him, he asked to be patched through to his wife, Jan, seven months pregnant with their first child. Both knowing that no one ever survived two consecutive nights on Everest, they talked for hours, discussing among other things what she would name their baby. "Don't worry about me too much," he finally told her. Then he turned off his radio.

One who literally came back from the dead was 50-year-old wealthy Dallas pathologist Seaborn Beck Weathers. When rescuers reached him, he was unconscious. The rules of the mountain are tough: you rescue only those who have a chance. So they left Weathers' lifeless body. A few hours later Weathers awakened. "I was lying on my back in the ice," he remembers. "I was colder than anything you can believe. My right glove was gone; my hand looked like it was molded of plastic." Weathers lay there for what felt like an hour, imagining that any minute someone would come by and waken him from his unpleasant dream, before it dawned on him that he was about to die. "I could see the faces of my wife and children pretty clearly. I figured I had three or four more hours left to live, so I started walking." Hours later people in the high camp were astonished to see a zombie-like figure staggering down the slope toward them. Face blackened from the sun, arms held rigidly outward, eyes closed to slits, Weathers had refused to die.[1]

Death is a fact of life on Everest. More than 140 have died trying to reach the top, or else succeeded and died while returning back down the mountain. Their bodies, zipped for eternity into bright nylon parkas, lie where they fell, enduring reminders to every carefully outfitted climber who passes by that the mountain can still win.

Solomon will tell us, though, that death is a fact of life wherever you are, whoever you are. Whether good or evil, we all will die (Eccl. 9:1-3). What's more, life is as uncertain as death is certain. Like the sobered Everest climbers who trudge by the bright parka-covered bodies of those who didn't make it, death is impossible to ignore. "The living know they will die" (verse 5), Solomon says candidly. He doesn't mince any words about it. In fact, for Solomon the contemplation of death gives us the wisdom to live. Listen to what he says in chapter 7: "It is better to spend your time at a funeral than at festivals. For you are going to die and it is a good thing to think about it while there is still time" (verse 2, TLB). The contemplation of death gives us the wisdom to live!

Live Dogs and Dead Lions

Here's what Solomon has in mind. First, as long as life continues, we have hope for meaning and purpose. It's interesting how he puts it. An ancient proverb familiar to him but not to us said: "A live dog is better than a dead lion" (Eccl. 9:4). It doesn't have the full ring of truth in our day as it had back then. "Today, our pets are pampered. They are treated like luxuries. They are fluffed up, pedigreed, and respected like human beings—some are treated *better* than we treat humans. They sleep on our beds. Some of them actually eat at our tables."[2]

Once I visited a couple in Maryland. They had showed some interest in our church, so I stopped by to get acquainted. Happy to see me, they invited me into the kitchen, where they were eating supper. I glanced at the huge plates of spaghetti and meatballs and also eyed the dog, a large blond poodle. She was sitting on the table eating a plate of spaghetti. "Don't mind Schotzy," I heard the wife say as I beat back feelings of nausea. "She thinks she's a cat."

So what? I thought to myself. *I'd die before I let even my cat eat on the table with me.*

In Solomon's day, though, "dogs were diseased mongrels that ran in packs through city streets. People feared them."[3] Much like the mangy old dog I saw in Odessa, Ukraine. It was dirty and nearly hairless with scabs and oozing sores all over. Running along the street, looking for food, it approached me for a handout. I instinctively wanted to keep my distance.

Nevertheless, Solomon says that a live dog is better than the king of the jungle who's dead. Can you guess why? It's easy—"because the king of the jungle, if he's dead, has no hope. As long as there's life, there's a dream, there's the anticipation of a new plan, there's love, there's purpose. In one word, along with life comes the presence of *hope.*"[4] The reality of death emphasizes the opportunity life still provides.

I believe Solomon may have been talking about himself. After all, he was king of Israel, ruler of his jungle, but his life had collapsed into despair. He felt more like one of those sickly mongrel dogs. Why should he go on? "I hated life, because the work that is done under the sun was grievous to me," he confesses (Eccl. 2:17, NIV). Life had become so painful that he said, "I congratulated the dead who are already dead more than the living who are still living" (Eccl. 4:2). Ellen White tells us that "gloomy and soul-harassing thoughts troubled him night and day. For him there was no longer any joy of life or peace of mind, and the future was dark with despair."[5]

On their way out the door one Sabbath after worship a couple told me that they hated life. One of my associates had just preached a sermon comparing Judas and John. The couple identified with Judas. Deep down inside, they blurted out, they loved evil like Judas had. Darkness rather than light. They felt helplessly trapped in their life patterns and circumstances. That same week I had read a review on HBO's new movie about Marilyn Monroe—a classic story of an actress who wanted the love of all because she remained at her core a pained and lonely soul. That particular week also witnessed the suicide of one of the Navy's top admirals, Jeremy Boorda. Ground down by a host of pressures at home and at work, Boorda took his life rather than face queries by *Newsweek* about his right to wear two combat medals.

Life can get us down. A dead lion can look pretty good at times.

But while life is uncertain and death is certain, while life is painful and death seems sweet release, Solomon's unstinting advice is "Choose life!" A live dog is better than a dead lion, because even when you're living a dog's life, there's still hope. The lowest of the animals alive, Solomon reasoned, is better than the highest dead.[6]

I believe Solomon is telling us that "there is a difference between submitting to existence and choosing to live. Life is not what happens to us while we wait to die. Truly living is a choice."[7] Pain is inevitable, but misery is optional. As long as life continues, we have hope for meaning and for change. Furthermore, life is a precious gift, an important responsibility.

Bungee Jumping at 100

Did you see the amazing TV story of the zest for life displayed by an old guy named S. L. Potter? It was his one hundredth birthday. His idea of celebrating a century of life was to bungee-jump off a 210-foot tower. Potter's children, ages 68 to 74, vehemently opposed the idea, but Potter climbed up the 210-foot tower and leaped. His first words when he got off the cord? "Give me back my teeth!" Life was still wide open at 100.

Then there's the picture I saw in *Bike Magazine*. Mark Cosslett rigged two bungee ropes to his bike and rode off Hanging Rock in the Blue Mountains of Australia. He was glad he thought of two ropes. One rope hooked on his handlebars and snapped, making a sound like a gunshot. With only one rope left to take the blow, Cosslett fell about 100 feet when he had planned to drop only 70. Fortunately the other rope performed as planned, and Cosslett was alive and well when he sent in his incredible picture.[8]

Life is to be chosen, and fully lived, Solomon says. Here's how he puts it in chapter 9, verses 7 through 10: "Go to it then, eat your food and enjoy it, and drink your wine with a cheerful heart" (verse 7, NEB).

"Always be dressed in white and never fail to anoint your head" (verse 8, NEB).

"Enjoy life with the woman you love" (verse 9).

"Whatever task lies to your hand, do it with all your might; because in Sheol, for which you are bound, there is neither doing nor thinking, neither understanding nor wisdom" (verse 10, NEB).

I like that: "Go to it, then!" In other words, seize the ordinary little mundane, humdrum occasions in each day, and find satisfaction in them. Let the little things, the simple things, fill your life with goodness. Besides that, let every day be a special day. Sweeten it with some perfume and dress as if it's special. And don't forget to find pleasure and satisfaction in the primary relationships of life—your spouse, kids, and friends. As Leo F. Buscaglia says: "Death is a challenge. It tells us not to waste time. . . . It tells us to tell each other right now that we love each other."[9]

Finally, throw your heart into everything you do. Live with a passion. Work with a passion. Play with a passion. Love with a passion. Life is a gift. And when it's gone, there's no more love, thought, or activity of any kind. *Now* is the time to live! *Today* is when you have life!

This is no humanistic or secular hedonistic ethic of "Have a blast while you last." No "Life's short, play hard" Reebok kind of advertisement. No "Go for it because this is all you're ever gonna get" philosophy. Nor is it like the little children's book you can buy at Barnes and Noble titled *Lifetimes: The Beautiful Way to Explain Death to Children* (by Bryan Mellonie and Robert Ingpen). It tells in pictures and words the cycle of birth and death of our plant and animal world. Finally at the end it includes people in the cycle. People too are born, live, and die. Its conclusion? There are birth and death, and in between is living. That's it! Just living.

Get Purpose

Yes, Solomon is talking about living. But it is living life with hope and with moral purpose. Living life with profound spiritual meaning. That little phrase "for God has already approved your works" (Eccl. 9:7) is an important one. It gives a vital clue. The *Good News Bible* puts it this way: "It's all right with God." In fact, that's what God wants us to do: live life with our whole heart. After all, it is God who gives life (Eccl. 5:18, 19). At death the spirit returns to God, who gave it (Eccl. 12:7).

Solomon has in view here the Creator God. Because life is a gift from God, to be alive is to share that which distinguishes God from all creation. God is the "living God." The ability to enjoy life and to find meaning and purpose in it is an incredible gift of divine ennoblement (Eccl. 5:19). God gives us life, and He empowers us to live it fully, responsibly, with meaning, purpose, and a sense of wellness.

The book of Ecclesiastes declares, "Take life as a gift from God's hand, and receive God's plan and ennoblement to enjoy your life." At one time Solomon would not have been able to say that about his life, but he found meaning for life again in the living God. Here was hope for forgiveness, for renewal, for God's empowering grace, for meaning and purpose—hope for life.

When Seaborn Beck Weathers came to after lying unconscious for hours—nearly frozen to death on that wind-whipped subzero icy slope of Mount Everest—the vivid image of his family filled his mind.

He started walking. With the faces of his family vividly in mind, Weathers refused to die!

It was ultimately the love and grace and enabling power of the living God vividly in mind that enabled Solomon to refuse to die. To choose life. To realize that a live dog has hope, that the living God was there for him.

As long as there is life, there remains hope for meaning, for change, and for relationship with God. Solomon says seize life and live it for the glory of God. As long as you have breath, live it for Him. That's the heartbeat of Scripture: "I call heaven and earth to witness against you today, that *I have set before you life and death,* the blessing and the curse. So *choose life* in order that you may live, you and your decendants, by loving the Lord your God, by obeying His voice, and by holding fast to Him; for this is your life and the length of your days" (Deut. 30:19, 20).

Jesus said: "I came that they may have life, and have it abundantly" (John 10:10, RSV). That choice lies before you right now. The same hope. The same meaning. The same grace. The same living God. Choose life!

---

[1] "High Risk," *Newsweek,* May 27, 1996, pp. 50-57; "Death Storm on Everest," *Time,* May 27, 1996, pp. 36-38.

[2] C. Swindoll, *Living on the Ragged Edge,* p. 261.

[3] *Ibid.*

[4] *Ibid.*

[5] E. G. White, *Prophets and Kings,* p. 76.

[6] E. Young, *The Meaning of Life,* p. 189.

[7] *Ibid.,* pp. 188, 189.

[8] *Bike Magazine,* May 1996, p. 38.

[9] As quoted by J. Canfield and M. V. Hansen in *A Second Helping of Chicken Soup for the Soul,* p. 131.

13

HELLO FROM HEAVEN! AND THE NECROPHILIC ROMANCE

For the living know they will die;
>*but the dead do not know anything,*
>*nor have they any longer a reward,*
>*for their memory is forgotten.*
Indeed their love, their hate, and their zeal have already perished,
>*and they will no longer have a share in all that is done*
>*under the sun.*
>>>*—Ecclesiastes 9:5, 6*

And the sixth angel poured out his bowl upon the great river,
>*the Euphrates;*
>*and its water was dried up,*
>*that the way might be prepared for the kings from the east.*
And I saw coming out of the mouth of the dragon
>*and out of the mouth of the beast and out of the mouth of*
>*the false prophet,*
>*three unclean spirits like frogs;*
>*for they are spirits of demons, performing signs,*
>*which go out to the kings of the whole world,*
>*to gather them together for the war of the great day*
>*of God, the Almighty.*
>>>*—Revelation 16:12-14*

It was a heart-gripping blockbuster. Netting $500 million in the first year, the film was one of those touchie-kissie-sweetie Hollywood movies that puts a lump in your throat and makes you want to hold on tight to that special person you love. A yuppie, killed in a mugging, learns in afterlife that a friend set up his death. Now his girlfriend is in trouble. He's got to get to her before it's too late. But how? Fortunately, he encounters a woman who has been faking that she's a medium, but now realizes she really is one. His message gets through. The vapory fellow and his corporeal love finally meet again. There's one last dance. By this time tears fill your eyes. You struggle with the tender, sweet, romantic relationships of life, the gripping pain of separation, and the meaning of death—which here isn't really death at all. In fact, lovers don't really die; they just hang around in thin air. Patrick Swayze, Demi Moore, and Whoopi Goldberg played their parts well in the highly popular romantic comedy-drama titled *Ghost*.

Spellbound by the blockbuster success of *Ghost,* Hollywood producers loaded the pipeline with a dozen movies in 1991 alone about the afterlife. Films such as *Bill and Ted's Bogus Journey*—two suburban dudes who die, go to hell, and come back in a rock band. Or *Defending Your Life*—an ad executive dies, goes to Judgment City, successfully defends himself, and falls in love. Or *The Rapture*—a mother murders her daughter, but the child returns to warn her mom about the coming apocalypse, complete with four horsemen in blinding yellow light. Another one, called *Switch,* portrays the story of a male chauvinist who dies, gets sent to purgatory, and finally returns to earth as a blond woman to pay for his sins.

The hero for the nineties has often been the dead. Or nearly dead. Or just back from the dead. What is interesting is Hollywood believes that death could be both fun and meaningful at the same time.[1] It's part of the new search for spirituality that has captured America.

Have you seen the book *Hello From Heaven!* by Bill and Judy Guggenheim? It presents a new so-called field of research that it labels "After-death communication." "After-death communication"

(ADC) occurs when a person supposedly receives direct and spontaneous contact from a deceased family member or friend without the use of psychics or mediums. One may sense a presence, hear a voice, feel a touch, or smell a fragrance. There may be partial appearances, full appearances, symbolic gestures, etc. The Guggenheims have documented the ADC experiences of more than 2,000 people, and estimate that nearly 50 million Americans have had an ADC experience.

The back of the dust jacket speaks of "fascinating modern-day evidence of life after death." "Comfort and emotional support for those who are grieving." "Hope for those who yearn to be reunited with a loved one who has died." "Inner peace for those whose hearts and minds are awaiting the good news."[2]

The gist of all this and much more that we find in the media—from *Reader's Digest* to *Life* magazine to the tabloids hanging by the checkout counters—is that there is no death. It does not exist and is not our last enemy. Rather, it's our friend, something that we needn't fear. When we die we don't vanish. There's a soul that's you or I, and it will always be there. Larry Gordon, chief executive of the movie production company Largo Entertainment, puts it this way: "People are looking for something that makes them feel good. We all want to believe that death isn't so bad."[3]

Enchanted Ground

But that's not how Solomon sees it. He too lived in a world that wanted to believe that death wasn't all that bad. His contemporaries down in Egypt were busy building and stocking their tombs for the next life. All the pagan religions around his kingdom were steeped in afterlife theologies and occult experiences, as were most of his wives. And yet, Solomon would categorically go against the grain of contemporary culture—both his and ours—and declare: "The living know that they will die; but the dead do not know anything, nor have they any longer a reward, for their memory is forgotten.

Indeed their love, their hate, and their zeal have already perished, and they will no longer have a share in all that is done under the sun" (Eccl. 9:5, 6).

I've had people tell me that Solomon was talking about life lived *under the sun,* not life after death. That what he says is true for down here, but not up there. Also they have tried to convince me that Solomon's theology was Old Testament and incomplete. Let's listen carefully, though, to what Solomon actually says. He contrasts the living and the dead (something Scripture does repeatedly), so if life is life, then, death is death. The living know something the dead don't. Furthermore, all love, hate, and zeal perish when a person dies. It's in that context that he says they no longer have a share in all that takes place under the sun. They can't, because they're dead.

We must remember too that Solomon obviously had the book of Genesis in mind as he wrote Ecclesiastes. That's why he would tell us that "the fate of the sons of men and the fate of beasts is the same. As one dies so dies the other; indeed, they all have the same breath and there is no advantage for man over beast. . . . All go to the same place. All came from the dust and all return to the dust" (Eccl. 3:19, 20). And to "remember Him [your Creator] before the silver cord is broken and the golden bowl is crushed, the pitcher by the well is shattered and the wheel at the cistern is crushed; then the dust will return to the earth as it was, and the spirit will return to God who gave it" (Eccl. 12:6, 7).

The Hebrew word for breath and spirit is the same, *ruach.* Solomon could see God forming man out of the dust of the ground and blowing into his nostrils the breath of life. Man became a living being (Gen. 2:7). The combination of the body and the breath of life made Adam a living being. When you die, that breath goes back to God, who gave it in the first place, Solomon says. And when it does, you no longer know anything. You can't love or hate or have any more zeal to do anything more. Returning to the dust, you're simply no longer in existence.

But Solomon could hear too the "primal lie" that the serpent hissed in Eden: "You surely shall not die!" (Gen. 3:4). Every generation has picked up that lie and kept it alive. "Death is hot" today because we're headed toward the final generation, in which what you believe about death may very well determine your eternal destiny. "I saw coming out of the mouth of the dragon and out of the mouth of the beast and out of the mouth of the false prophet, three unclean spirits like frogs; for they are spirits of demons, performing signs, which go out to the kings of the whole world, to gather them together for the war of the great day of God" (Rev. 16:13, 14).

John writes about a master delusion that gathers the whole world against God. At its heart is that primal lie "You surely shall not die!" Quoting the passage in Revelation, Ellen White writes: "Satan has long been preparing for his final effort to deceive the world. . . . Little by little he has prepared the way for his masterpiece of deception in the development of spiritualism. He has not yet reached the full accomplishment of his designs: but it will be reached in the last remnant of time."[4]

She warns about spiritualism as much as she does about the Sabbath/Sunday issue, because spiritualism is going to have a major role in Satan's final deception. His master delusion of spiritualism assumes some highly subtle and diverse forms: NDEs (near-death experiences), OBEs (out-of-body experiences), ADCs (after-death communication), New Age teachings, mystical healings, altered states of consciousness, Eastern meditation, astrology, horoscopes, the rising fascination with angels, and apparitions of Mary. Two *Time* magazine year-end cover stories say volumes about the current fascination with the occult. "New Age of Angels: 69 percent of Americans believe they exist. What in heaven is going on?" *(Time,* Dec. 27, 1993) and "Mary: Handmaid or Feminist?" *(Time,* Dec. 30, 1991). The number of books on, interest in, and encounters with angels (only good angels, of course) constantly increases. More and more people around the world worship Mary or see Marian apparitions. Pope John Paul II saw her intercession as having brought Communism's defeat. It's all part of a master delusion.

Testing the Spirits

Ellen White put all this in context when she wrote in *The Great Controversy* that many will find themselves ensnared through belief that spiritualism is a merely human imposture. When brought face-to-face with manifestations that they cannot but regard as supernatural, they will be deceived and will accept the phenomena as God's great power. In other words, our modern Western society that now rejects God and the Bible because of the empirical scientific method will come full circle, because with their senses they have now encountered the supernatural. Ellen White adds: "He [Satan] has power to bring before men the appearance of their departed friends. The counterfeit is perfect; the familiar look, the words, the tone, are reproduced with marvelous distinctness."[5]

Elisabeth Kübler-Ross, renowned Swiss therapist and expert on death and dying, had an ADC that convinced her that death does not exist.[6] *Hello From Heaven's* coauthor Bill Guggenheim writes that he always figured the dead had ceased to exist until he started researching ADCs. Now he's a believer. And so were the people in the 350 stories told in his book.

In her book *Testing the Spirits* Elizabeth Hillstrom, associate professor of psychology at Wheaton College, points to what she sees as "a discernable shift away from traditional Western systems of thought—including Christianity, Judaism and secular materialism—and toward a worldview that is nonlogical, subjective, experience-oriented and mystical. This newer perspective bears some resemblance to New Age thought but is less extreme, less obviously tied to Eastern religious dogma, more eclectic and much more compatible with important Western beliefs. Thus it appeals to a much broader range of Westerners.

"This new mystical outlook . . . assumes that the spirit realm is real, including the spiritual aspects of human nature and the existence of other spiritual beings. It exalts human nature. . . . It anticipates hidden powers in the human psyche like clairvoyance, mental telepathy and the ability to heal and to contact the realm of spirits. Its notion of life after death is linked with universalism (the belief that everyone goes to heaven regardless of their beliefs) and sometimes with reincarnation. Finally, this new perspective minimizes the importance of rationality and objectivity and relies heavily on subjective inner experiences as sources of ultimate truth."[7]

I see two significant points to this shifting worldview: (1) a nonlogical experience-oriented thinking that relies heavily on subjective inner experiences as sources of ultimate truth—not the Bible, not facts, but experience; and (2) a universalism that views no difference between good and evil, righteous and wicked—both have life after death. Those who have gone to the grave unprepared appear to return. They claim to be happy, setting God's law aside and rejecting the need for grace, the deity of Jesus, even the cross. Many of those allegedly contacted "dead" were never Christians to begin with, and those who reported meeting the dead rarely become committed Christians as a result of their NDE. Instead, they become suspicious of religious sectarianism. In other words, not only do we live *after* we die, but we don't need to be born-again committed Christians *before* we die.

Why the shift? Hillstrom links it to extraordinary supernatural or mystical experiences that have been occurring with greater frequency in recent years (NDEs, OBEs, UFOs, New Age movements, mystical healings, etc.). She cites a 1984 Andrew Greely poll that showed a full 42 percent of Americans saying they have been in contact with the dead (a 25 percent increase since 1973). A 1990 Gallup poll supports the growing shift toward mystically tinged experiences.[8] People who have been confronted by the supernatural have new memory experiences that change their perceptions of reality.

Hillstrom is simply saying what Revelation and *The Great Controversy* have already warned our final generation about. The whole world will be duped. She's simply confirming the more detailed outline of issues Ellen White penned more than 100 years ago.

Can Adventists be duped too? Or do we know better? I wonder sometimes.

A young Andrews University friend of ours (who grew up in a denominational employee's family, going through our elementary and academy system) shared how she had gone to one of those Hollywood afterlife movies. Almost as an afterthought in our conversation, she shared, "You know, I'm not sure about all this. I could almost believe we're still alive when we die. It seems so real, so right!"

We need to listen up! "Except those who are kept by the power of God, through faith in His word, *the whole world* will be swept into the ranks of this delusion."[9]

"All whose faith is not firmly established upon the word of God will be deceived and overcome."[10]

But it's more than merely knowing the Word. It's believing it, hiding it in our heart, and being careful about what we expose ourselves to, not just this one subject of death and afterlife, but other issues as well. We must realize how our defenses can slowly break down.

While we can't deny the supernatural experience that we or someone else may have, we can with Bible in hand question its interpretation. I'm concerned about a generation of Adventists who may not be all that sure anymore. We may think we know what we believe until confronted by some supernatural phenomenon that we hadn't expected. Again, Hillstrom clarifies the issue: "Today's mystical experiences affect individuals by challenging their worldview. These experiences contradict the basic tenets of materialism, and most are also unacceptable by strict biblical standards. Yet to those who experience the events they seem extraordinarily real and meaningful. To reconcile the contradictions this creates, people must either discount their experiences or modify their beliefs. Unfortunately, it appears that many people are modifying their beliefs rather than questioning the validity of their experiences."[11]

The world's ready to be deluded. All around the globe, in almost every culture, faith, and country, events are preparing people for the grand lie. It's a "dark strategy to snare an entire civilization, Christian and pagan, Western and Eastern, first world and third world, educated and illiterate, rich and poor."[12]

They're reading from the same page, says Clifford Goldstein: "Secularist, Protestant, Catholic, Jew, Muslim, Buddhist, Hindu—because of their misunderstanding of the state of the dead, none has protection against Satan's last-day deceptions. From Billy Graham to the Dalai Lama, from the mullahs of Iran to Catholic priests in South America, all are susceptible to Satan's most subtle, powerful, and universally accepted deception that 'you shall not surely die.'"[13]

Before the Silver Cord Is Broken

Solomon gives us a clue for the final showdown just before Jesus comes again. It's a truth that will see us through if we never let it go. "The living know they will die; but the dead do not know anything" (Eccl. 9:5). And so, he says, "Remember Him [your Creator] before the silver cord is broken. . . . Fear God and keep His commandments, because this applies to every person. For God will bring every act to judgment, everything which is hidden, whether it is good or evil" (Eccl. 12:6-14). Death is death. There's no universalism. One must choose rightly, today. Remember God! Enter into obedient relationship with Him.

Every night I felt her searching eyes, saw her questioning face. Ekaterina was a short, plumpish, elderly woman attending my evangelistic crusade in Odessa, Ukraine. Each evening she would come and listen, then wait patiently in line to ask me questions. Every evening she would literally scan my eyes. I could tell by the way she looked at me that she was thinking, *Who is this American claiming to know the Bible? Are these things he is telling us really true? Can I trust him? How does this square with what the priests have told me?*

Ekaterina never took her eyes off me as I answered her questions. My messages on the Sabbath, baptism, the Second Coming, and the pagan traditions that have crept into the Christian church clearly rattled the faithful Orthodox woman. Nothing disturbed her more, though, than what I said about death and our absolute need for Jesus alone. Orthodox Christians adore the virgin Mary. Mary is at the

135

center of their religious experience, holding an incredible intercessory position. Everywhere you go in the Ukraine you encounter icons expressing Mary's pivotal position in both Orthodox faith and life. "Mother and child" icons are very common. In such statues or paintings Mary looms large and Jesus is always little. Just a baby, still. I did see one icon that depicted Jesus as a fully grown man, but He was a miniature man in the hands of a full-sized Mary. The subtle implication in such depictions, whether intended or not, is that Mary is the one to reckon with. She's the real celestial power broker.

You can imagine Ekaterina's frustration, then, as I explained that the Bible teaching on death meant heaven has no saints to which we can bring our prayers for intercession. That includes the virgin Mary. Like all others, the mother of Jesus is asleep in the grave waiting for the resurrection. Unable to help anyone with their prayers, she has no life in herself to give. But Jesus is different. As High Priest, Jesus ever lives to make intercession for us (Heb. 7:25). Furthermore, Jesus is the resurrection and the life (John 11:25). Our hope is in Him alone, not in any saint. Nor in the immortality of the soul.

Sadly, Ekaterina found that truth about Jesus hard to accept and finally returned to her belief in the soul's immortality and the efficacy of an interceding Mary.

In the early 1960s Oscar Cullmann rocked the scholarly world with his little book *Immortality of the Soul or the Resurrection of the Dead?*[14] His was a simple thesis that offended many—and still does. The Christian hope for life after death resides in the biblical teaching of bodily resurrection of the dead, not in the Greek pagan idea of universal immortality.

I would add that at the heart of this Christian hope of bodily resurrection stands Jesus. Our hope is not in bodily resurrection itself, but in Jesus, *who is* the resurrection and the life. We do not trust in a concept, but a person, the resurrected Lord Jesus Christ who sits at the right hand of the Father, ever living to make intercession for us. He is the one who beckons our faith and alone gives true promise. It is to Him that you are invited to come and find life beyond the grave.

Popular author and Episcopal priest Robert Farrar Capon puts a creative spin on the existential angst so often felt over this controversial subject. Speaking of the wild enthusiasm of the God who makes all things new by bringing them out of nothing; whose cup of tea is lostness, deadness, uselessness, and nothingness, he writes: "One of the worst things that ever happened to the church was the importation into its doctrinal structure of the Greek notion of the immortality of the human soul. Because do you know what that did? It persuaded us that nothingness is something that God has no serious use for anymore. Once the church had enticed us with the notion of a finer, more spiritual part of our nature—a beautiful butterfly of a soul which, once it is released from the nasty cocoon of the body, will shoot up to heaven by its own rocketry—we convinced ourselves that *we would never have to be nothing again.* Which gave us a mere half-reason for needing Jesus as our resurrection: we would never be more than half dead. We turned Jesus into a kind of celestial mechanic who would bolt repaired bodies back onto souls that had made it to the heavenly garage on their own. The Protestants among us refused to talk about the soul after death, and the Roman Catholics got the bright idea of running the soul through the car wash of purgatory before the Last Day. All of us were agreed, though, that there would never be a time when we were truly dead—when we had gone all the way back into the nothing from which we came." [15]

Capon goes on to say that when he urges people to chuck the immortality of the soul as a piece of antigospel baggage, they worry. They tell him, "Look, this is 1997. What about 2097? If I don't have an immortal soul, and the Rapture doesn't happen in the meantime, where will I be then?"

His response?

"You look: what are you worried about? You were nothing in 1797, and it hasn't bothered you so far. Why should it bother you now? Can't God do the same trick a second time? . . . Nothing is all he needs for anything." [16]

All we need for life after death is Jesus. All Jesus needs to awaken us from death's silent sleep is nothing but nothing—except our unswerving faith in Him alone as the Resurrection and the Life right now while we still have breath.

<hr>

[1] "Hollywood Goes to Heaven," *Time,* June 3, 1991, pp. 70, 71.

[2] Bill Guggenheim and Judy Guggenheim, *Hello From Heaven* (New York: Bantam Books, 1995).

[3] "Hollywood Goes to Heaven."

[4] E. G. White, *The Great Controversy,* p. 561.

[5] *Ibid.,* p. 552.

[6] Elisabeth Kübler-Ross, *On Life After Death* (Berkeley, Calif.: Celestial Arts, 1991), pp. 31-36.

[7] Elizabeth L. Hillstrom, *Testing the Spirits* (Downers Grove, Ill.: InterVarsity Press, 1995), pp. 9, 10.

[8] *Ibid.,* pp. 16, 17.

[9] White, p. 562. (Italics supplied.)

[10] *Ibid.,* p. 560.

[11] Hillstrom, p. 216.

[12] Dwight K. Nelson, *Countdown to the Showdown* (Fallbrook, Calif.: Hart Research Center, 1992), p. 100.

[13] Clifford Goldstein, *Day of the Dragon* (Boise, Idaho: Pacific Press Pub. Assn., 1993), pp. 109, 110.

[14] Oscar Cullmann, *Immortality of the Soul or the Resurrection of the Dead? The Witness of the New Testament* (London: Epworth Press, 1958).

[15] Robert Farrar Capon, *The Foolishness of Preaching* (Grand Rapids: William B. Eerdmans, 1998), p. 24.

[16] *Ibid.,* p. 25.

14

BIRTHDAY, DEATHDAY, AND THE SCENT OF YOUR NAME

A good name is better than a good ointment,
And the day of one's death
is better than the day of one's birth. . . .
The end of the matter is better than its beginning.
—Ecclesiastes 7:1-8

Not far from Lincoln, Kansas, a strange group of tombstones stand in an old graveyard. A farmer and self-made man named John Davis erected them. Davis started out as a lowly hired hand and by sheer determination and frugality managed to amass a considerable fortune in his lifetime. In the process, however, the Midwestern farmer did not make many friends.

When his wife died, Davis erected an elaborate statue in her memory. He hired a sculptor to carve a monument that showed them both sitting together on a loveseat. He was so pleased with the result that he commissioned another statue—this time depicting himself, kneeling at her grave, placing a wreath on it. That impressed him so greatly that he had a third monument made. It depicted his wife kneeling at his future grave site and also placing a wreath. Since she was no longer alive, he had a pair of wings added to her back, giving her the appearance of an angel. One idea led to another, until he'd spent nearly a quarter million dollars on the monuments to himself and his wife!

Whenever someone from town would suggest he might help with a community project—such as a hospital, a park and swimming pool for children, or a municipal building—the old miser would frown, set his jaw, and shout back, "What's this town ever done for me? I don't owe this town nothin'!"

Through the years Davis used up all his money on stone statues and other selfish pursuits. Finally he died at the age of 92, a grim-faced resident of the poorhouse. But his monuments? Strangely, they are slowly sinking into the Kansas soil, fast becoming victims of time, vandalism, and neglect, sad reminders of a self-centered, unsympathetic life. In the course of time they too will be gone.

By the way, few people attended John Davis's funeral. It is reported that only one person seemed genuinely moved by any sense of personal loss. He was Horace England, the tombstone salesman.[1]

Solomon challenges us with the character monuments we are building in the eyes of others and God. He presents what seems a strange piece of wisdom when taken in pieces, but profound truth when viewed as a whole: "A good name is better than fine perfume, and the day of death better than the day of birth" (Eccl. 7:1, NIV). It's one of those pithy "better than" proverbs that jars your mind to grasp its "real" meaning.

A Name for Ourselves

During Solomon's day people would anoint themselves with sweet-smelling perfumes or ointments to hide the odor of unwashed bodies and to display their ability to afford expensive perfumes. You could pick such people out of the crowd anywhere, their aromatic scent catching everyone's attention. But a good name, Solomon reasoned, goes further than a cosmetic cover-up. While fragrant perfume is good, a good name is better. Good reputation is better than good scent. Then Solomon seems to throw us a curve. He joins the idea of fragrant perfume and a good name with another: "The day of one's death is better than the day of one's birth." Why? "Because between birth and death, we make a name for ourselves."[2] At birth we can only speculate about what a person will be like or become, but chances are that on the day of their death, we will *know* for sure. The day of death is better than the day of birth, Solomon said, "because on the day of death, all the returns will be in. The person will be known for who he or she really was."[3]

Solomon was contrasting two significant days in human experience: the day a person receives his or her name, and the day when that name shows up in the obituary column. The life lived between those two events will determine whether that name leaves behind a loving fragrance or a foul stench. It comes down to the question of who we really are in the eyes of others and God. In the process Solomon gives us some wisdom nails to assure that we not only have a good name while we are alive, but end up with a good name—whether at our funeral or in the final judgment.

First, *internals are better than externals when it comes to having a good name.* One of the anecdotes I enjoy telling is the surprise love story about John Blanchard and Hollis Maynell. Blanchard was an Army serviceman who stumbled across Maynell's name while browsing in a Florida library. Taking a book off the shelf, he found himself intrigued, not with the words of the book, but with the notes penciled in the margin. The soft handwriting reflected a thoughtful soul and insightful mind. In the front of the book he found the previous owner's name: Miss Hollis Maynell. With time and effort he located her address in New York City. He wrote her a letter introducing himself and inviting her to correspond. The next day he was shipped overseas for active duty in World War II. During the next 13 months the two grew to know each other through the mail. Each letter seemed like a seed falling on a fertile heart. A romance was budding.

Blanchard asked for a picture, but she refused. Hollis felt that if he really cared for her, it wouldn't matter what she looked like. When the day finally came for him to return from Europe, they scheduled their first meeting—7:00 p.m. at Grand Central Station in

New York. "You'll recognize me," she wrote, "by the red rose I'll be wearing on my lapel." So at 7:00 Blanchard waited in the station looking for a girl he loved, but whose face he'd never seen.

Here's how Blanchard tells it: "A young woman was coming toward me, her figure long and slim. Her blond hair lay back in curls from her delicate ears; her eyes were blue as flowers. Her lips and chin had a gentle firmness, and in her pale-green suit she was like springtime come alive. I started toward her, entirely forgetting to notice that she was not wearing a rose. As I moved, a small provocative smile curved her lips. 'Going my way, sailor?' she murmured.

"Almost uncontrollably I made one step closer to her, and then I saw Hollis Maynell.

"She was standing almost directly behind the girl. A woman well past 40, she had graying hair tucked under a worn hat. She was more than plump, her thick-ankled feet thrust into low-heeled shoes. The girl in the green suit was walking quickly away. I felt as though I was split in two, so keen was my desire to follow her, and yet so deep was my longing for the woman whose spirit had truly companioned me and upheld my own.

"And there she stood. Her pale, plump face was gentle and sensible, her gray eyes had a warm and kindly twinkle. I did not hesitate. My finger grasped the small worn blue leather copy of the book that was to identify me to her. This would not be love, but it would be something precious, something perhaps even better than love, a friendship for which I had been and must be ever grateful.

"I squared my shoulders and saluted and held out the book to the woman, even though while I spoke I felt choked by the bitterness of my disappointment. 'I'm Lieutenant John Blanchard, and you must be Miss Maynell. I am so glad you could meet me; may I take you to dinner?'

"The woman's face broadened with a tolerant smile. 'I don't know what this is about, son,' she answered, 'but the young lady in the green suit who just went by, she begged me to wear this rose on my coat. And she said if you were to ask me out to dinner, I should go and tell you that she is waiting for you in the big restaurant across the street. She said it was some kind of test.' " [4]

Had Blanchard turned his back on the unattractive, he would have missed the love of his life. Internals are better than externals when it comes to making a name for yourself. What we are in our heart and life, and how we treat others, is more important than what we wear or what we have, the degrees behind our name, or what our hair looks like. Like perfume that flows out with fragrance to those around us—our principles, our convictions, our words, our actions, our lifestyle, our manners, and our methods of dealing with people—all leave impressions about ourselves. Perfumes elicit response. They invade and permeate the space of others. Likewise, our character constantly creates an atmosphere about us—saturating the inner space of those around us, whether family, friends, or a watching world.

A good name is a man or woman who has influence and character. A woman who changes lives. A man who impacts others. That good name comes because they have nurtured the habits of the heart. They have developed integrity, compassion, kindness, truthfulness, liberality, joyfulness, and contentment.

To this Solomon adds that *ending well is critical when it comes to developing a good name.* Look again at verse 8: "The end of a matter is better than its beginning; patience of spirit is better than haughtiness of spirit." A great beginning is important, but many who have had great starts have experienced terrible finales. Starting well is good—but finishing well is critical. We need to persevere. A good name is not a right, but a gift offered on the basis of a lengthy history of reliable contributions to the lives of others. It implies the esteem of the community, having elicited trustworthiness, gratitude, respect, and enduring remembrance.

The WSBT-TV news in South Bend, Indiana, told the story of the Studebakers, an impoverished family with disabilities among both parents and children, who raised money to eat and pay their bills by collecting discarded cans and bottles. On one of their daily forages they stumbled across a wallet with nearly $3,000 in it. A real find? The answer to prayer? A way out of debt or the means to fix the car? No! They immediately went to the police with their find and returned the wallet complete with cash to its rightful owner. When word got out, people started asking, "Why didn't they keep it? Finders keepers, losers weepers, right?" That's not how the impoverished family thought. "It was the right thing to do," they stated. Their honesty and integrity literally captured the imagination of the people of South Bend, bringing an outpouring of gifts and help that far exceeded the $3,000.

The family's decision tells me two things. First, decisions like that don't come in a moment. Character develops by a series of decisions. We build our name though a lengthy history of sustained and reliable contributions to the lives of others. Second, ordinary people like you and me can have good names. Ordinary people can be individuals who make an impact. But there must be commitment and faithfulness. Ellen White says that "character is revealed, not by occasional good deeds and occasional misdeeds, but by the tendency of the habitual words and acts."[5]

A woman entered an airport gift shop with an hour or so to spare before her flight. She purchased a newspaper and a small package of cookies and then settled into a chair near the appropriate gate to wait. Opening her paper, she began to read. A man sat down opposite her, resting his briefcase and a cup of coffee on the small table between them. He opened his paper too.

As she read, she reached for a cookie from the bag in the center of the table and popped one into her mouth. A few minutes went by, and she took another cookie—but they had been moved. The package, now half empty, was sitting on top of the briefcase belonging to the man beside her. *How unbelievably rude!* she thought, sliding the cookies back to her side of the table and taking another one.

Then she heard the rustle of cellophane and watched him remove the last cookie from the package. It was too much. Putting down her paper, she glared at the seemingly nonrepentant cookie thief, who shrugged his shoulders, broke the cookie in two, and offered her half!

Angrily gathering her things, she gave him one final withering stare and headed for the other side of the waiting area. Her fury did not subside until a half hour into her flight, when she reached into her bag for a pen and pulled out . . . her unopened package of cookies![6]

Perspective is critical. Every decision we make reflects our understanding of reality. And so we come to Solomon's final nail: *Today is the moment of opportunity for making sure your name is a good name.* It is the recurring theme of Ecclesiastes, the critical perspective every one of us needs. Each day we have a chance to make sure our name is a good one. "Remember Him [your Creator] before the silver cord is broken," Solomon pleads (Eccl. 12:6).

Between birth and death we establish a name for ourselves. On the day of death all the returns will be in. We will be known and seen for who we really are in the eyes of both others and of God. So today we must achieve a good name. Today we must enter our inner private world of thought and attitude, priority and virtue, and ask ourselves whether or not we are keeping up or slacking off. Both beginning well and staying at it so we end up well.

Counting the Returns

In June of 1996 our world watched as the Israeli elections between Shimon Peres and Benjamin Netanyahu reached a virtual dead heat. Ultimately, less than 1 percent of the voters (30,000 votes out of 3 million) decided it. Everyone waited till the day after the election, when less than 100,000 absentee ballots remained to be counted. Only when all the returns were in could it be said for sure who had won. Which name would cast its influence over Israel's life, and perhaps history, during the years to come?

People evaluate our name every day of our lives. Like opinion polls, they are accumulating views of who we really are and what we really stand for. The day is coming when all the returns will be in on us! Because "God will bring every act to judgment, everything which is hidden, whether it is good or evil," we read (Eccl. 12:14).

"So live," as the old saying goes, "that when death comes the mourners will outnumber the cheering section." In light of eternity, I think we should put it the opposite way: "So live, that when death comes, the cheering section will outnumber the mourners." That is, in the eyes of a watching universe the host of evil will mourn their failure at your good name, but God and the host of unfallen worlds will celebrate because you've made it.

Neither is a product of our own power. A good name among our fellow human beings or a good name before God in the final judgment is not within our ability. We can't originate it, develop it, or sustain it. We can only choose it, then open ourselves to those inner character issues that God is speaking to us about. Holy Spirit power in our inner private world will transform us. That's what's at the heart of the "better than" proverbs. Choice. Priority. Character. Solomon sets it all in the context of a relationship with the living God: "The conclusion, when all is heard, is: fear God and keep His commandments, because this applies to every person" (verse 13). Knowing God, loving Him, yielding to Him is the secret to the unlocking of His name-building grace.

Ellen White tells us that "when the love of Christ is enshrined in the heart, like sweet fragrance it cannot be hidden. Its holy influence will be felt by all with whom we come in contact."[7] And as Paul says: "Thanks be to God, who always leads us in His triumph in Christ, and manifests through us the sweet aroma of the knowledge of Him in every place. For we are a fragrance of Christ to God among those who are being saved and among those who are perishing" (2 Cor. 2:14, 15). Now, that's real perfume!

---

[1] "Monuments," as told by Charles Allen in *Stories for the Heart: 110 Stories to Encourage Your Soul,* comp. Alice Gray (Gresham, Oreg.: Vision House Publishing, 1996), pp. 77, 78.

[2] E. Young, *The Meaning of Life,* p. 150.

[3] *Ibid.*

[4] "Promises to Keep," *Focus on the Family* magazine, June 1989, pp. 21, 22.

[5] Ellen G. White, *Steps to Christ* (Mountain View, Calif.: Pacific Press Pub. Assn., 1956), pp. 57, 58.

[6] As told by Young, pp. 147, 148.

[7] White, p. 77.

DEAD FLIES
FLOATIN' IN YOUR TEA

Dead flies make a perfumer's oil stink,
so a little foolishness is weightier than wisdom and honor.
A wise man's heart directs him toward the right,
but the foolish man's heart directs him toward the left.
—Ecclesiastes 10:1, 2

While in Odessa, Ukraine, on a six-week-long evangelism assignment, I lived in the home of a wonderful Ukrainian family. On one occasion, though, I had an unexpected decision to make.

I love fresh cherries. So when my host set out a large bowl for supper, I dove right in. I must have eaten two dozen or more before I saw the little guys—little plump white worms munching away on the same cherries. From the inside out! Quickly I checked a few more cherries, being careful not to let my hosts notice. All the cherries had worms.

Then it sunk in! Every cherry I had popped in my mouth had included one of those dinky little cherry lovers. Suddenly I didn't like cherries anymore! I mean, what would you do? Try to forget about what you now know and keep on eating? Would you take the time to pick out every one of those little critters—in front of your hosts? Or would you just find something else to eat and hope no one offered you more cherries?

Imagine being served a cool glass of iced tea in a fancy restaurant. You add lemon and sugar and stir it all up just right. Then, as you lift it to your lips for that first sip, your eye catches something that's not quite right. You find a dead fly floating in the lemon pulp on top. (We used to freeze flies in ice cubes for just such momentous occasions of sibling harassment!)

What would you do? Just pick it out and drink on? Would you be satisfied if your waiter, after being called over, simply took a spoon and removed the offending insect? Certainly not! You would want a new glass of tea, even if the fly only "swam" in a small portion of it. Right?

Say you buy an expensive bottle of perfume. Opium, Chloe, or some of that Victoria's Secret stuff. When you open its box at home, you lift it up to enjoy the hue cast by light refracting through its delicate ornate bottle. What catches your eye immediately is a dead fly drifting up and down in the perfume inside. After all that expense, would you keep it or take it back? Shouldn't expensive perfume be fly-free?

It's amazing how just a little problem or a minor flaw, a little scratch, a missing piece, a broken part, a slight discoloration—some dead flies—can make something very undesirable.

Solomon confronts us with the incredible power of little things to undo much larger things. "Dead flies make the perfumer's sweet ointment turn rancid and ferment; so can a little folly make wisdom lose its worth" (Eccl. 10:1, NEB). Something extremely small, such as a dead fly, is enough to ruin a jar of precious perfume in the eyes of a buyer. Enough to cause a foul odor distorting the gentle fragrance of the perfume.

So with a little foolishness in our lives! A little touch of evil. A little trace of error. A little pinch of private sin. All of it can contaminate the whole. One error of judgment, one false belief, one yielding to temptation, one bad habit, one unprincipled friend, one hidden desire, one unsavory attitude, one unconfessed sin, one misplaced loyalty—just one dead fly can smear our name, negate our witness, undo our inner private world, and undermine our connection with God.

Which Way Are You Going?

Solomon has already compared a good name to fragrant per-fume (Eccl. 7:1). Now he connects perfume imagery with wisdom. Here Solomon tells how fragile wisdom is. In his mind wisdom is synonymous with a good life, a godly life, a character formed in re-lation to God. But it doesn't take much to corrupt it. Errors in judg-ment threaten wisdom constantly. Folly is so powerful that a little of it can overwhelm large amounts of wisdom. So Solomon gives us three more nails to hang our commitment to moral excellence on.

First, *know where your heart is headed!* "A wise man's heart di-rects him toward the right, but the foolish man's heart directs him toward the left" (Eccl. 10:2).

One of the joys of owning a new car is that it has no steering pull to the right or left that demands your constant effort to keep the car centered in its proper lane or easily negotiate turns. You can take a new car out on a straightaway, take your hands off the steering wheel, and it will continue going straight ahead. Even when you ac-celerate, it glides along dead on. With time, however, most cars de-velop steering pull problems. Mechanics identify two kinds of steering pull problems—torque steer and memory steer. They are not tire-related problems that we can easily solve with new tires. Instead, they reflect how a car has been broken in and aged. Torque steer is most noticeable under acceleration and goes away when you shift into neutral. It comes from such things as worn bushings and tired suspension. Memory steer is when your car pulls in the same direction as the last turn. It almost always results from binding in the suspension on that side of the car.[1] The bottom-line question is al-ways "Why does the car pull in a certain direction, and what can be done to fix it?"

Our lives can develop steering pull as well. We can head in pre-dictable moral/spiritual directions whenever life and its problems ac-celerate. Often we move in the same direction as the last moral/spiritual turn.

Solomon is talking about the habits of our heart, the moral and spiritual orientation of our inner private world. Does it go to the left, or does it go to the right? *Right* in this verse represents that which is worthy of our effort and pursuit. *Left* is anything unworthy. In Hebrew thinking the right was the good and strong while the left stood for the bad, the weak, and the sinister. Imagery depicting the right hand as where God is fills Scripture. Psalm 16:8 says that the Lord "is at my right hand," and Psalm 121:5 states that "the Lord is your shade on your right hand." Jesus is said to have "taken his seat at the right hand of the throne of the Majesty in the heavens" (Heb. 8:1). Thus *right* is a picture of protection and power and the very presence of God.

In Solomon's thinking the wise person goes God's way while a fool doesn't. A fool plays in the *left* zone. The latter craves the excitement and the adventure of wrong. A wise man or woman gravitates toward the good, and the foolish toward the bad. *Right* and *left* are the two spiritual directions for the heart.

Such spiritual direction isn't referring to a shallow, off-the-top-of-one's-head, or seldom-made mistake. The occasional good deed or bad deed. No! It has in mind a deep-seated, heartfelt pursuit in a given moral or spiritual direction. Solomon was concerned with the inclinations of the heart—the center of one's life, the master control within us that governs the issues of life. Be careful for your heart. Know where it is leaning.

Solomon's second nail goes something like this: *Weigh the issues carefully!* "Even when the fool walks along the road his sense is lacking" (Eccl. 10:3). A few years back a friend of mine told me about a guy who worked for him. My friend owned a log cabin home business for which he hired a few unskilled workers to cut and plane cedar logs. The employee was new on the job. His job required no specific intelligence, just some common sense. All he had to do was feed the stock through the milling machines at an even pace. His boss had clearly spelled out all the proper safety equipment and precautions.

One afternoon the employee stood looking at the saw blade

spinning on the table saw. Intrigued by the blur created by the whirling blade, he reached down and touched it! Zing! His finger was gone and blood spattered everywhere. "I just wanted to see what it felt like," he told my friend on the way to the emergency room.

"What in the world was he thinking?" his boss asked me. The fact is that the employee wasn't thinking. And so is the way of the fool. He's not really considering what he's doing. According to Solomon, the fool "misses his mind." In other words, his brains are in neutral and he's out to lunch.

Scripture defines "folly" as a lack of good common sense, of foresight, and a failing to realize the consequences of a stupid act before it occurs. Here Solomon tells us that the heart of folly is the idea that "little things" aren't that important. Fools say to themselves, "What difference does it make?" or "It doesn't matter." The problem is that they never take the time to really know for sure. Yes, many little things in life don't really matter. While that may be true, whom is it true for? What are those little things? Who determines what they are? And who says they don't matter—our friends, our secular world, or God? Or is it ourselves?

Just some little O-rings caused the mammoth *Challenger* space shuttle to explode within seconds of takeoff. A few neglected little maintenance items and a slight bending of the rule with some oxygen canisters in the cargo area sent a ValuJet flight flaming from the sky into a Florida swamp. Little things are especially important when it comes to moral and spiritual issues. Everything has value in light of eternity. It was just a little fruit from the tree of knowledge of good and evil. It was just a few rich delicacies from Nebuchadnezzar's table. Maybe a little pork and a few social drinks, that's all. And the ark was about to fall when Uzzah reached up to touch it. It was just a little anger and striking a rock that kept Moses from the Promised Land. A little withholding of money that killed Ananias and Sapphira.

Solomon is telling us we must put on our thinking caps. We need to wrestle with principles and the deeper issues of our faith and what God is calling us to do and be. He wants us to understand and know why little things do make a difference. Each of us needs to weigh the issues carefully and see them as God views them. Apparently insignificant unwise behavior can ruin eternity.

Sports fans will always remember Steve Lyons as the baseball player who dropped his pants. Posterity could have regarded him as an outstanding infielder, as the team member who played every position for the Chicago White Sox. He was a favorite of the fans as the player who high-fived the guy who caught the foul ball in the bleachers. Baseball histories could have recorded him as an above-average player who made it with average ability. But he'll go down as the player who dropped his pants on July 16, 1990.

The White Sox were playing the Tigers in Detroit. Lyons bunted and raced down the first-base line. Knowing it was going to be tight, he dove at the bag. Safe! The Tigers' pitcher disagreed. He and the umpire got into a shouting match, and Lyons stepped in to voice his opinion. Absorbed in the game, Lyons felt dirt trickling down his pants. Without missing a beat he dropped his britches, wiped away the dirt, and . . . uh-oh! Twenty thousand jaws hit the bleachers' floor. And as you can imagine, the jokes began. Women behind the White Sox dugout waved dollar bills when he came onto the field. "No one," wrote one columnist, "had ever dropped his drawers on the field. Not Wally Moon. Not Blue Moon Odom. Not even Heinie Manush." Within 24 hours of the "exposure," Lyons received more exposure than he'd gotten his entire career: seven live television and approximately 20 radio interviews. "We've got this pitcher, Melido Perez, who earlier this month pitched a no-hitter," Lyons stated, "and I'll guarantee you he didn't do two live television shots afterward. I pull my pants down, and I do seven. Something's pretty skewed toward the zany in this game." Fortunately for Steve, he was wearing sliding pants under his baseball trousers. Otherwise the game would have been rated R instead of PG-13.[2]

This brings us to Solomon's third nail: *Choose as if everybody's watching!* Here's how he puts it: "Even when the fool walks along the road his sense is lacking, and he demonstrates to everyone that he is a fool" (Eccl. 10:3). Poor judgment is never a well-kept secret. The very way a fool walks announces that he lacks wisdom. Bad moral and spiritual and other everyday life decisions announce our status as a fool.

I stated earlier (chapter 1) that Ecclesiastes' pithy proverbs were no mere Gumpisms—the wit and wisdom of an idiot. Rather, they are inspired insights into the heart of what life is all about. One of the tidbits in the little book *Gumpisms: The Wit and Wisdom of Forrest Gump* states that "being a idiot is a lot of fun when ain't nobody lookin'"[3] That agrees with a piece of graffiti someone scrawled on a wall: "A man is who he is when he is alone." Solomon reminds us that we can never really hide who we are inside. It ultimately comes out. Many of us do all kinds of things in private—behind closed doors, on vacation, with select friends—that we would never do in the open. We figure no one will ever know, that it doesn't really matter or make a difference. It's incredible what many of us are in the privacy of our own home or when no one else is around.

Years ago I became impressed with the thought that a host of angels and a watching God know what we really are. While people may not be able to sit back and laugh at the foolish things I do, the host of evil can. And in time people will too. Solomon says that in the end everyone will discover the truth. In time it will become clear as we walk down the street. During the final judgment "God will bring every act to judgment, everything which is hidden, whether it is good or evil" (Eccl. 12:14). When weighed against eternity, our poor decisions about little things, or one little bit of evil in our private world, will announce our status as a fool. So choose as if everybody's watching. What people see and remember about us is important. And what God observes is even more vital!

If There Were a Thousand Steps

A little bit of corruption in our private world can contaminate the whole. It can ruin wisdom, heading us off in the wrong direction and causing us to overlook how important little things are. It is never a well-kept secret. So know the direction of your heart. Weigh the issues carefully.

Ellen White tells us that "it is a perilous thing to allow an unchristian trait to live in the heart. One cherished sin will, little by little, debase the character, bringing all its nobler powers into subjection to the evil desire. The removal of one safeguard from the conscience, the indulgence of one evil habit, one neglect of the high claims of duty, breaks down the defenses of the soul and opens the way for Satan to come in and lead us astray."[4]

"The removal of one safeguard from the conscience, the failure to fulfill one good resolution, the formation of one wrong habit, may result not only in our own ruin, but in the ruin of those who have put confidence in us."[5]

With Solomon she says: "There is not an impulse of our nature, not a faculty of the mind or an inclination of the heart, but needs to be, moment by moment, under the control of the Spirit of God."[6]

It is time to get a grip on our hearts and our lives and decisions. We must take a good long look at how consistent we are in our commitment to Jesus and just how fully we honor Him in our lives. Are we playing the fool or walking in godly wisdom?

A young man sat alone on the bus and most of the time just stared out the window. In his mid-20s, he was nice-looking with a kind face. His dark-blue shirt matched the color of his eyes, and his hair was short and neat. Occasionally he would look away from the window, and the anxiety on his young face touched the heart of the grandmotherly woman sitting across the aisle. The bus was just approaching the outskirts of a small town when she felt so drawn to the young man that she scooted across the aisle and asked permission to sit next to him. After a few moments of small talk about the warm spring weather, the young man blurted out, "I've been in prison for two years. I just got out this morning and I'm going home." His words tumbled out as he told her he was raised in a poor but proud family and how his crime had brought his family shame and heartbreak. During the whole two years he had not heard from them. He knew they were too poor to travel the distance to where he had been in prison, and his parents probably felt too uneducated to write. When no replies came, he stopped writing.

Three weeks before his release he had desperately written one more letter to his parents, telling them how sorry he was for disappointing them and asking them for their forgiveness. He went on to explain about his approaching release from prison and that he would take the bus to his hometown—the one that went right by the front yard of the house where he grew up and where his parents still lived. In his letter he said he would understand if they wouldn't forgive him. Wanting to make it easy for them, he asked them to give him a signal that he could see from the bus. If they had forgiven him and wanted him to come back home, they could tie a ribbon on the old apple tree that stood in the front yard. If the signal wasn't there, he would stay on the bus, leave town, and be out of their lives forever.

As the bus neared his street, the young man became more and more anxious to the point that he was afraid to look out the window, because he was so sure there would be no ribbon. After listening to his story, the woman asked simply, "Would it help if we traded seats and I sat near the window for you?" The bus traveled a few more blocks, and then she saw the tree. She gently touched the man's shoulder and choking back tears said, "Look! Oh, look! The whole tree is covered with white ribbons."[7]

Some of us look at our hearts and see a pulling to the left. We recognize that we haven't been all that careful with the little things. Having played the fool to our family, our friends, and our church, we're embarrassed and want to hide. Dead flies float in our tea! But God promises He is there to receive us, to forgive us, to give us wisdom if we will but fear Him. His renewing grace is always available.

As always, Max Lucado puts it succinctly: "If there are a thousand steps between us and God, He will take all but one. He will leave the final one for us. The choice is ours." It is always a matter of choice, even for little things like dead flies.

[1] Paul Wiessler, "Solving Steering-Pull Problems," *Popular Mechanics,* March 1996, pp. 96-99.

[2] "Moon Man," *Sports Illustrated,* Aug. 13, 1990, pp. 58-63, as told by M. Lucado, *In the Eye of the Storm,* pp. 247, 248.

[3] W. Groom, *Gumpisms,* p. 59.

[4] E. G. White, *Patriarchs and Prophets,* p. 452.

[5] *The Seventh-day Adventist Bible Commentary,* Ellen G. White Comments (Washington, D.C.: Review and Herald Pub. Assn., 1976), vol. 2, p. 1004.

[6] White, *Patriarchs and Prophets,* p. 421.

[7] "The Signal," in *Stories for the Heart,* pp. 83, 84.

UNABOMBER, SOLITAIRE, AND *CHEERS*

Then I looked again at vanity under the sun.
There was a certain man without a dependent,
> *having neither a son nor a brother,*
> *yet there was no end to all his labor.*
Indeed, his eyes were not satisfied with riches
> *and he never asked,*
>> *"And for whom am I laboring and depriving myself of pleasure?"*
This too is vanity and it is a grievous task.
Two are better than one because they have a good return for their labor.
For if either of them falls,
> *the one will lift up his companion.*
But woe to the one who falls when there is not another to lift him up.
Furthermore,
> *if two lie down together they keep warm,*
> *but how can one be warm alone?*
And if one can overpower him who is alone, two can resist him.
A cord of three strands is not quickly torn apart.

> **—*Ecclesiastes 4:7-12***

Ted Kaczynski was an eccentric Montana loner whom no one would miss if he vanished for weeks at a time. When he did show up in the little town of Lincoln, you could smell him coming. Saturated with wood smoke, dressed in black or sometimes fatigues, he pedaled a one-speed bike thrown together out of spare parts. He didn't say much. Often he wouldn't even finish a sentence. Once in town he'd buy a few supplies, read in the library, and then disappear again for six months. Townspeople called him "the hermit on the hill."

All the dogs hated Kaczynski. They'd chase him, bark at him, growl whenever he walked or rode his bike. For 25 years he lived in a little home made out of plywood with an outhouse out back and a root cellar below. He lived a grubby, lonely subsistence in one of the most rugged regions of North American outback. It is the kind of place you're likely to see grizzly bears more often than another human being.

For all practical purposes, Kaczynski had erased himself from human society. But in reality he hadn't—or couldn't. For nearly two decades he spent his time bombing innocent people he didn't know. He was a calculating serial terrorist we now know as the notorious Unabomber. Twenty-three victims felt the passion of his anger, alienation, and estrangement. Some died. Others were maimed for life. The arrest and disclosure of his life stirs the imagination with images of a shy brilliant boy who became a pathologically reclusive man. Kaczynski was someone who had no friends, no allies, and no networks, and whose inner psyche couldn't handle the very thing he sought—loneliness and isolation.

A former Harvard classmate of Kaczynski's, Gerald Burns—now a poet—says the news of Kaczynski's arrest hit him hard. He has written a poem, "Letter Bomb for Ted," that takes a sympathetic view of the man many would consider to be a criminal psychopath. "Please don't make him sound like a monster," Burns said. "He really was a gentle person."[1]

But obviously somewhere along the way the shy gentle person's psyche snapped. You can go only so long without a network of friends and allies. Being a loner has a definite downside.

That's where Solomon brings us in this passage. While down in the marketplace he noticed a solitary man hard at work. The king discovered that the man had no brothers or sisters, no sons or daughter, no partners to help him in his business. Nor did he desire any help. An independent man, he was obviously driven. *And never satisfied.*

"Why is he working so hard? Why doesn't he slow down and enjoy life?" Solomon mused. "This is very sad and senseless," he said to himself (see Eccl. 4:7, 8). Solomon's point is that the man had isolated himself. Rich, he had probably withdrawn himself from others so no one would make demands on him. He intentionally built a wall around himself. In the end he was empty, lonely, and hurting.

You can play solitaire only so long without its getting to you! And you can go only so long without friends. Isolation has unhealthy consequences. "We need each other," Solomon declares. "Two are better than one" (verse 9). Without each other, unhappy things happen. People cannot function effectively without deep links to others. He gives us a few nails to hang on to.

Cheers for the Neighborhood Bar

First, two are better than one, "because together they can work more effectively" (verse 9, TEV). "Two can accomplish more than twice as much as one, for the results can be much better" (TLB). Solomon has mutual effort in mind.

Watching the world-champion U.S. women's rowing team propel their pencil-thin boat through the water is awesome. They glide along, covering 2,000 meters, or 1.25 miles, in less than seven minutes. It's like watching a warm knife cut butter. When they train for the Summer Olympics, they are filled with one passion—take the gold. That means incredible mutual effort both physical and mental. Can you imagine eight different people with the same stroke? One can get lulled by their rhythms—the catch, draw, release of their oars—eight bodies moving as one. They must row between 38 and 48 strokes a minute. Their heart rates hit 190 by the second stroke and stay there till they cross the finish line.[2]

How many of us don't like help or advice, or would rather do things on our own? Many of us don't like accountability. Too individualistic, we don't want the hassle of working with others, whether it be at home, at church, at work, or in the community. But Solomon tells us that mutual effort pays off. We gain perspective by having somebody at our side. Besides, we gain advantage, because we can accomplish so much more when we work together.

Our family loves mountain biking. Each of us sports one of those flashy multigear sweat machines that will literally leave you exhausted, and could hospitalize you. We find nothing more thrilling or scary than tearing through the woods trying to negotiate our way through trees that are just 15 inches apart or keep balance (and your heart out of your throat) while ripping down the side of a hill you wouldn't even walk down.

The sport has been the most challenging for our son Evan. Not only is he young in years and small of stature, but his bike is a tad bigger than it should be. He does a pretty good job at it, nevertheless. Every once in a while, though, he doesn't make a turn and runs off into the woods or bushes or down a bank—reminding us of those eccentric characters in Richard Scarry's books who have one creative catastrophe after another. And his brothers? They just zip by. No one stops to help (except Mom or Dad). It's not only embarrassing to skid off into the woods; it's discouraging as well, not to say anything about bruises and pain. We have a really experienced biking friend who often rides with us. When he does, he will stay with Evan and coach him along. Evan's confidence and skill have raised considerably because of his help.

This brings us to Solomon's second observation that two are better than one, because "if one of them falls down, the other can help him up. But if someone is alone and falls, it's just too bad, because there is no one to help him" (verse 10, TEV). In the NASB he uses some pretty strong language here: "Woe to the one who falls when there is not another to lift him up." Woe means anguish, grief, heartache, misery, sorrow, and loss. Solomon has mutual support in mind. In times of personal failure—when we fall on our faces or have gotten into trouble—we need someone to keep us from getting too down. Someone to help us see light again and that there's hope and possibility.

Who catches you when you fall? Are you likely to aid someone else when they stumble or just ride by them? Some married partners have a search-and-destroy-the-adversary kind of relationship rather than a support-and-encourage, affirming one. It's tragic, yet true, that some are married to mates who do not lift up their companion. Churches are known for shooting their own wounded. In Galatians the apostle Paul writes: "Dear brothers, if a Christian is overcome by some sin, you who are godly should gently and humbly help him back onto the right path, remembering that next time it might be one of you who is in the wrong" (Gal. 6:1, TLB).

A popular TV sitcom hit of the 1980s received nominations for more than 110 Emmy awards and won 28. It pulled 150 million viewers on its May 1993 final episode. Its Boston location is a popular attraction for the thirsty and hungry. The comedy, starring Ted Danson, Shelley Long, and Kirstie Alley, explained itself in the words of its theme song that spoke of wanting to go somewhere where everybody knows your name.

In *The Edge of Adventure* Keith Miller writes: "The neighborhood bar is possibly the best counterfeit there is to the fellowship Christ wants to give His church. It's an imitation, dispensing liquor instead of grace, escape rather than reality, but it is a permissive, accepting, and inclusive fellowship. It is unshockable. It is democratic. You can tell people secrets and they usually don't tell others or even want to. The bar flourishes not because most people are alcoholics, but because God has put into the human heart the desire to know and be known, to love and be loved, and so many seek a counterfeit at the price of a few beers. With all my heart I believe that Christ wants His church to be . . . a fellowship where people can come in and say, 'I'm sunk!' 'I'm beat!' 'I've had it!' "[3]

I believe Solomon himself sought the companionship of friends to cut the edge off his own loneliness (Eccl. 2:7, 8). He surrounded himself with people who could cater to his whims, provide for his needs, and do whatever he said. Solomon sought social gatherings, parties, wherever people were. The king was a sanguine, a party animal looking for companionship to solve his loneliness problem. As a result, he went where the people were. And so do people today. Church, bar, games. The question is Do they find supportive, encouraging, open, accepting people? One of the principles of church growth involves creating a climate of open and accepting relationships. Growing churches understand that people have different levels of relationships: the crowd level, the membership level, the fellowship level, and the ministry level. You can be part of the crowd who comes and goes, or even be an official member without having any significant relationships.

Furthermore, Solomon tells us that two are better than one, because "if it is cold, two can sleep together and stay warm, but how can you keep warm by yourself?" (Eccl. 4:11, TEV). His third nail? Mutual encouragement and support are helpful when we're vulnerable. Who encourages you? Whom do you encourage? Let's consider some vulnerable times just in case you can't think of any examples: The first day on a new job or at school. Going to make things right with someone after you've really messed up. Filing papers for a divorce. Going to an empty home after the funeral. When you're about to get that expected bad news from the doctor. When you've been laid off or your son gets arrested.

Every time I've been to the Ukraine someone has told me lurid stories about the local Mafia. I've heard tales about innocent travelers who have lost their cars, money, and luggage somewhere along the border of Poland and the Ukraine or the Ukraine and Russia. Carefully planted individuals at the border will note how much money you declare, or what kind of car you are driving. They will alert their friends ahead. Then a few miles down the road you suddenly find yourself surrounded by armed thieves and left walking or dead. One pastor told of being stopped by Mafia border bandits.

They demanded money and his car. Miraculously they let him go after he forcefully declared himself an Adventist pastor whose money and vehicle were needed for the Lord's work. He drove away with a signed piece of paper telling Mafia cronies down the road (who might intercept him again) that he had already been stopped and that they should leave him alone.

On one of my trips to the Ukraine I traveled alone. I carried in my possession some large amounts of money that I was to deliver personally to various church leaders and individuals. Honesty at a customs check means full declaration—writing down what you have with you. But I wasn't too nervous, knowing that when I arrived at the airport in Odessa several people and their cars would be waiting for me. My Ukrainian friends know the principle in life (the fourth nail) that two are better than one, because "if one can overpower him who is alone, two can resist him. A cord of three strands is not quickly torn apart" (verse 12). I like how *The Living Bible* puts it: "One standing alone can be attacked and defeated, but two can stand back-to-back and conquer; three is even better."

A friend recently walked down a dark street one night in a neighborhood he always thought of as risky even in the daylight. As he went along, he kept looking to the right and to the left for any movement in the shadows. At the same time he would glance back to see if anyone might be following him. All of a sudden, *bam!* He walked right into a streetlamp. As he fell backward in pain, he thought for sure someone had mugged him.

"One standing alone can be attacked and defeated, but two can stand back-to-back and conquer; three is even better." Nothing can be more true in spiritual and moral warfare. How much we need each other. We must have the accountability of others around us. When we're alone, we're open to temptations and thoughts we would easily dismiss if someone were with us. Isolated, we're vulnerable to all kinds of things. As a result we need the prayers of others, their words of exhortation, and their perspective that might say: "You know, I think this is an enemy from Satan's domain."

Solomon outlines for our modern age the unhealthy consequences of isolation, the essential benefits of relationships, and the absolute necessity to be a friend and be befriended. People need people. Faithful friends who stand by our side are a precious gift in life. For whatever reason we might fall, we need someone to pick us up, to believe in us. We crave the warmth of others, both emotionally and physically. Part of being human is receiving and giving help to each other.

Survival goes hand in hand with fellowship. As Charles Swindoll says: "One plus one equals survival." Mutual effort, mutual support, mutual encouragement, and mutual strength mean getting in touch, feeling the hurts, and being an instrument of encouragement. These imply opening up, sharing our hurts, and receiving encouragement.

Ellen White sees incredible evangelism potential in these kinds of caring and supportive relationships. She suggests there would be a hundred baptisms where there is now just one.[4]

When Paul Villiard was young, his family had one of the first telephones in his rural neighborhood. He remembers the polished oak case and the shiny black receiver on the side of the box and even their number: 105. Villiard was too little to reach the telephone, but used to listen with fascination when his mother talked to it. Once she lifted him up to speak to his father, who was away on business.

Then he discovered that somewhere inside that wonderful device lived an amazing person. Her name was "Information Please," and there was nothing she did not know. His mother could ask her for anybody's number. When their clock ran down, Information Please supplied the correct time. Villiard's first personal experience with this genie-in-the-receiver came one day while his mother was visiting a neighbor. He was playing at his dad's basement toolbench and whacked his finger with a hammer. The pain was terrible, and the boy had no one to give him sympathy. All he could do was walk around the house sucking his throbbing finger. Then he spied the telephone. Grabbing the footstool in the parlor, he climbed up and unhooked the receiver. "Information Please," he said into the mouthpiece.

A click or two, and a small clear voice spoke into his ear. "Information."

"I hurt my fingerrr," he wailed into the phone. That soft voice in his ear advised him to wrap his finger in ice, then offered words of comfort. After that, Villiard called Information Please for everything. She helped him with geography and arithmetic and told him what the chipmunk he caught would eat. The woman offered comfort, too, when his pet canary died. "Paul, always remember that there are other worlds to sing in," she said as he wept into the phone. She even helped him spell the word "fix."

Then Villiard's family moved to Boston, leaving him lonely for his mentor. Information Please belonged in that old wooden box back home. Somehow he never thought of trying the tall, skinny new phone that sat on a small table in the hall. Yet as he grew into his teens the memories of those childhood conversations never really left him. Often in moments of doubt and perplexity he would recall the serene sense of security he had when he knew he could call Information Please and get the right answer. He appreciated how patient, understanding, and kind she was to have wasted her time on a little boy.

A few years later, on his way west to college, Villiard's plane touched town in Seattle. He had about a half hour between connections, and he spent 15 minutes or so on the phone with his sister who lived there. Then, really without thinking what he was doing, he dialed his hometown operator and said, "Information Please."

Miraculously, he heard again the small clear voice he knew so well. "Information."

He hadn't planned it, but he heard himself saying, "Could you tell me, please, how to spell the word 'fix'?"

After a long pause, there came the softly spoken answer. "I guess," the woman said, "that your finger must have healed by now."

Villiard laughed. "So it's really still you. I wonder if you have any idea how much you meant to me during all that time."

"I wonder," she replied, "if you know how much you meant to

166

me? I never had children, and I used to look forward to your calls. Silly, wasn't it?"

Villiard told her how often he had thought of her through the years, and asked if he could call again when he was in the area.

"Please do. Just ask for Sally."

"Goodbye, Sally." It sounded strange for Information Please to have a name.

Three months later he was back in the Seattle airport. A different voice answered when he dialed Information, and he asked for Sally.

"Are you a friend?"

"Yes," he replied. "An old friend."

"Then I'm sorry to have to tell you that Sally had been working only part-time during the past few years because she was ill. She died five weeks ago." But before Villiard could hang up, she said, "Wait a minute. Did you say your name was Villiard?"

"Yes."

"Well, Sally left a message for you. She wrote it down."

"What was it?" he asked.

"Here it is, I'll read it. 'Tell him I still say there are other worlds to sing in. He'll know what I mean.'"[5]

When You're Down and Out

Back in the late 1960s and early 1970s our country found itself ripped apart by factions and turmoil surrounding the war in Vietnam and the values of our American society. Disillusioned young men and women were openly defiant and rebellious against the establishment. At the same time up-and-coming entrepreneurs, career people, and often mom and dad rejected the young people. We had a generation of lonely, forsaken, friendless young people who traveled the country in their buses, lived in the streets, and strummed their guitars through the night, higher than a kite on marijuana and finding closeness in free sex. Paul Simon, you may remember, gave them a song to sing in 1970. The song reassured them, telling them that when everything else fails and falls, when nothing but trouble loomed all around, one thing would get them through—a friend. That friend would be "like a bridge over troubled waters."

Later Chuck Swindoll asked, "Did you get that? Did you notice the writer's insightful words? He didn't say, 'I'll give you a book to read.' Neither did he say, 'I'll tell you what to do,' nor, 'I'll give you a job.' No. He said that when things get rough, 'I'll lay *me* down.' 'I'll comfort you.' 'I'll be your bridge.'"

Then he added, "There's no bridge quite like a friend, especially when you're forced to live on the ragged edge of troubled waters."[6]

Hopefully we have such a bridge or are such a bridge to others. For sure we have such a bridge in Jesus Christ! Jesus says: "I call you friends." "I will never leave you or forsake you." "I will not leave you as orphans." "I will come to you." "I will be with you."[7] Having become one with us in our sorrows and trials, He ministers for us in heaven. He is a bridge over troubled waters and has literally laid Himself down for us. Now He invites us to do the same for one another.

[1] "Probing the Mind of a Killer," *Newsweek,* Apr. 15, 1996, pp. 30-42; "Tracking Down the Unabomber," *Time,* Apr. 15, 1996, pp. 38-46.

[2] "8 Live Crew," *Time,* "Special Edition: The Summer Olympics," Summer 1996, pp. 76-79.

[3] Bruce Larson and Keith Miller, *The Edge of Adventure* (Waco, Tex.: Word Books, 1974), p. 156.

[4] "If we would humble ourselves before God, and be kind and courteous and tenderhearted and pitiful, there would be one hundred conversions to the truth where now there is only one" (Ellen G. White, *Testimonies for the Church* [Mountain View, Calif.: Pacific Press Pub. Assn., 1948], vol. 9, p. 189).

[5] Paul Villiard, "Information Please," *A Third Serving of Chicken Soup for the Soul* (Deerfield Beach, Fla.: Health Communications, 1996), pp. 14-18.

[6] C. Swindoll, *Living on the Ragged Edge,* p. 142.

[7] See John 15:14-16; Heb. 13:5; John 14:18; Gen. 28:15; Isa. 41:10.

17

WIRE WALKERS AND THE GHOST OF MIGHT-HAVE-BEEN

Cast your bread on the surface of the waters,
for you will find it after many days.
Divide your portion to seven, or even to eight,
for you do not know what misfortune may occur on the earth.
If the clouds are full, they pour out rain upon the earth;
and whether a tree falls toward the south or toward the north,
wherever the tree falls, there it lies.
He who watches the wind will not sow
and he who looks at the clouds will not reap.
Just as you do not know the path of the wind
and how bones are formed in the womb of the pregnant woman,
so you do not know the activity of God who makes all things.
Sow your seed in the morning, and do not be idle in the evening,
for you do not know whether morning or evening sowing
will succeed,
or whether both of them alike will be good.
—Ecclesiastes 11:1-6

W hen Philippe Petit first saw a sketch of the proposed 110-story New York World Trade Center in a dentist's office magazine, he ripped it out and threw it into a box he called "projects." That was 1968. As the World Trade Center towers neared completion in 1973, Petit's interest increased. In his opinion the two towering structures looked incomplete. They would remain so until connected by a wire walker's cable. Petit realized, though, that the twin towers' owners probably wouldn't see it that way. So his challenge was to smuggle a half ton of cable and related gear to the top of one tower, figure out a way to get the cable across to the other, then tighten it sufficiently to support 150 pounds of Frenchman carrying a 55-pound balancing pole.

They were the obvious challenges. But he faced still others, such as surviving the crosswinds to walk seven times across a cable strung 1,350 feet above lower Manhattan. The winds between the two towers are so turbulent that Petit was unable to find a helicopter pilot willing to fly him between them for a look. Then he had to deal with the natural sway in the towers and the stress it would put on his 21-ply, ⅞-inch cable. Wouldn't it snap like a cheap cotton thread? Of course there was the possibility of being nabbed before he got a chance to set foot on it. Then Petit would look like a fool and receive a fine.

Disguised as workmen, Petit and a helper managed to sneak up in a freight elevator to the top of the south tower. There they hid underneath the tarp on a steel beam until security guards finally left for the night. Posing as architects with briefcases, two other members of the crew made it to the top of the north tower. Pulling a crossbow from the briefcase, they shot a weighted nylon thread across the dark void. To it they attached a stronger cord. The next few hours of darkness they spent painfully inching the heavy cumbersome cable across the cord. Then they had to tighten it with a combination of muscle power, winches, pulleys, and a heavy-duty ratchet.

Just before sunrise, everything was nearly ready. As the large metal wheel of a nearby elevator began groaning beside him, bringing the day's first workers to the top, Petit gripped his 35-foot, 55-pound balancing pole in both hands and gingerly set one black-slippered foot on the cable. It trembled like a loose guitar string. He rose and steadied his pole, paused for a second, then placed his second foot irretrievably into the void. "Look! There's a tightrope walker!" shouted two of Petit's assistants from the street below as they pointed to his tiny silhouette in the sky. To the raised eyes of a fascinated world, Philippe Petit's seven crossings between the World Trade Center's towers—dancing, spinning, grinning, lying down in the middle—became a lasting metaphor for daring.[1]

If anyone has brought to life the wires we all might walk if only we dared, it's been Philippe Petit.

And that's where Solomon now brings us. To the wires we all might walk if only we dared. Solomon knew human nature well. He recognized our tendency to slip into routine, boring, and predictable ways. We usually think too small, dream too conservatively, and live too cautiously. Never reaching outside ourselves, we stay in our little clique and put off a new experience until we can afford it, or the time is right, or we're sure we can do it.

Fear keeps us in our comfort zones! One of those comfort zones is never really letting God have full control in our lives because we're not sure what will happen if we do. Solomon uses two life activities to make his point: the merchant sending out ships (Eccl. 11:1, 2) and the farmer sowing seed (verses 3-6). Both activities require a great deal of risk and faith, because neither the merchant nor the farmer can control circumstances. The ships might hit a reef, meet a storm, or be attacked by pirates and the cargo lost. Bad weather, blight, or insects might destroy the crop, and then all the farmer's labor would be in vain. However, if the merchant and the farmer waited until circumstances were ideal, they would never get anything done! Life has a certain amount of risk to it. That's where faith comes in.

Avoiding the Ghost of Might-Have-Been

So, Solomon says, don't sit around waiting for ideal circumstances. If you're looking for an excuse for doing nothing, you can always find one. Or if you're worried about the wind toppling a tree over you, or the clouds drenching you with rain, you'll never accomplish anything. There are some high and challenging wires you might walk, if only you dare. Nothing ventured, nothing gained! God may surprise you if you try. And so Solomon presents some well-driven nails to break us out of our comfort zones and help us walk some wires—whether in interpersonal relationships, our professional career, the use of our spiritual gifts, further spiritual growth, or whatever!

First, *instead of protecting yourself, release yourself to the challenge*. Here's how he puts it: "Cast your bread on the surface of the waters, for you will find it after many days" (verse 1). He's talking about a merchant sending his products through ships to carry on trade with foreign countries. Solomon understood the allusion. His ships sailed to Ophir, trading Israel's products for gold, ivory, spices, silver, apes, and baboons (1 Kings 10:22). His point, though, is that we need to let go before we can progress. "Release yourself to the challenge," he says. When it comes to walking wires in our moral and spiritual life, we have to let go. We have to reach the place inside where we say, "OK! I'll do it." Or "I'll trust God to do it with me!" Letting go can be a very emotional and scary thing.

I think of a retreat my staff and I used to introduce our congregation to the potential for small group ministry. We figured a weekend filled with small group experiences, complete with some deep spiritual sharing, would be a great way to stir imagination and interest. It worked. Out of the excitement and bonding of that weekend with nearly 100 in attendance, seven small groups were born.

One of the bonding activities we employed was called "the fall." Individuals would climb high up on a platform, straighten up like a soldier at attention, and fall back into the open arms of their comrades. Talk about trust. It is not as easy as you think. I was cheering people on when someone said, "Pastor Larry, when are you going to try it?" Good question! I had never done it before. It wasn't in my schedule. Now I was on the spot. So up I climbed and turned my back to the waiting hands below. Slowly I scooted my feet backward until just my toes held me on the edge. All I had to do was close my eyes and lean back, trusting those waiting hands. As I said, it's not as easy as you think when you've never done it before.

Elderly people often talk about things they regret not having done. Someone asked 85-year-old Nadine Stair from the hill country of Kentucky to look back over her life and reflect on what she had learned. With that touch of wistfulness that inevitably accompanies any statement beginning "If I had my life to live over . . . ," she said, "If I had my life to live over, I would dare to make more mistakes next time. I'd relax. I would limber up. I would be sillier than I have been on this trip. I would take fewer things seriously. I would take more chances. . . . I would eat more ice cream and less beans. I would perhaps have more actual troubles, but I'd have fewer imaginary ones. You see, I'm one of those people who live sensibly and sanely hour after hour, day after day. . . . I've been one of those people who never go anywhere without a thermometer, a hot water bottle, a raincoat, and a parachute. If I had it to do again, I would travel lighter."[2]

A sign along the Alaskan Highway reads: "Choose your rut carefully. You'll be in it for the next 200 miles."[3]

Solomon's second point has to do with ruts: "Divide your portion to seven, or even to eight, for you do not know what misfortune may occur on earth" (verse 2). In other words, don't put all your eggs in one basket. Wall Street calls it "diversification," and it is a good commonsense business practice. *Instead of doing just one thing, or the same old thing, diversify and expand your horizons, your opportunities, and your experiences.*

My family likes the Olive Garden restaurant. In fact, except for Pizza Hut, it's really the only place we ever go to eat out. And you know what? We usually order the same thing. It's a tasty rut, but still a rut. If you were to join us for a meal at home, you would find another predictable phenomenon. Each of us sits at the same place at the table, day after day, week after week, year after year. Just try to get us to relocate. Somehow it doesn't feel right, and it's hard to eat. Our reality is framed by seating. And conflict can break out over such a mundane thing.

Most of us wear the same style and color clothing we did decades ago. Our hair looks the same. We do the same old thing for vacations and on Saturday nights and birthdays. Such routine filters down to our spiritual life and our experience with church as well. We are comfortable only with the familiar and the safe—whatever doesn't call us to extend ourselves. Orthodoxy becomes equated with personal or congregational traditions and comfort zones. We become encased in private spiritual traditions with regard to worship styles or our potential as a congregation. The humdrum has made us its slaves.

"Get out of your rut!" Solomon urges. It is not a commentary on right or wrong. We can never remove ourselves from the routine of doing what is right and true. But we can live rightly in a new way, a fresh and better way. Solomon simply appeals to us to break out of any ordinary mindless routine that robs our life of imagination, freshness, and the potential for living life at its best and honoring God to our fullest.

To all this he adds a third thought: "Sow your seed in the morning, and do not be idle in the evening, for you do not know whether morning or evening sowing will succeed, or whether both of them alike will be good" (verse 6). In other words, *instead of drifting lazily along and doing the minimum, wholeheartedly pursue the opportunities that lie before you.*

I'm always amazed at the volume of life and work some people seem to experience and accomplish. Getting up early, they work hard all day. Traveling here and there, they take this class and read that book. Industrious people, they accomplish a whole lot more in a day than some of us get done in a week. Besides, they're interesting to be around. Solomon tells us to stretch, to reach, to take the challenge, to be downright bullish! Do the job at hand with thoroughness and industry both for ourselves and for God! We can do a whole lot more than we ever thought. It comes down to priorities, focus, and consistency.

See God Work in Your Life

During one of my trips to the Ukraine the airline I flew somehow messed up all my vegetarian meals. I was disappointed, to say the least. Since it would be difficult to ask for changes once in the Ukraine, I had to wait till my layover in Frankfurt on the way back. There I approached the ticket agent and shared my dilemma. I was not looking forward to the long flight back to the U.S. without vegetarian meals. Could she help? "I can't make a menu change at this late date," she said with a frown. "But how about first-class seating? It has a salad bar. Better yet, let's put you in the upper flight deck. There's a lot of food on that menu you could eat." So she bumped me up to first class in the upper flight deck. Just like that. I couldn't believe it. So for the first (and probably last) time in my life I got to experience what real flying is like. Extra-wide seats that recline. Godiva chocolates on demand. Attendants who wait on you hand and foot. Your own little flight bag with warm socks, mouthwash, and eye shades for sleeping. I felt like a fat cat, since I had always wanted to see what life was like up in the first-class upper flight deck.

Do you want to see God work in your life? Do you want to fly in the moral and spiritual upper flight deck? Solomon, I believe, gives us a formula: "The activity of God who makes all things" (verse 5). It is a simple phrase that lies in the middle of his flow of thought, one easily bypassed. What does it mean? If we do nothing, if we keep staring at the clouds, we will not know the work of God, who does everything. "These are astonishing words," Jacques Ellul comments. "God does everything, and yet, we must do something. God will cause one thing or the other to succeed, or both things. But you and I must do them! We cannot fail to act because God does everything."[4] In short, if we do nothing, we will be unable to perceive the work of God. We will never know His activity, because there may be no work of His in our lives to observe or experience.[5] Only in stepping out on the wire do we ever have the chance of seeing what God might do.

If we want to see God work in our lives, then we need to become bullish about doing the things He has called us to do. We need to step out and walk the wire by using our spiritual gifts, sharing our faith, giving liberally in tithes and offerings, and interceding on the behalf of others. Each of us must ask for the transforming power of the Holy Spirit and seek revival and reformation in our inner private world as well as in the fellowship of believers. Some of us dream about being different, about doing something for God. Perhaps we long to be stronger spiritually, to be persons of moral and spiritual impact, but it never happens. Why? Because we are not casting our bread, dividing our portion, sowing our seed.

Here's an incredible promise: if we take the risk and move forward, God may show His hand in blessing and opening doors. The problem, though, is that we cannot calculate just how God might choose to work or bless! We can't be presumptuous, because we don't know for sure what He may or may not do. The only thing we can be positive about is that moving ahead is better than staying put. It puts us in the position where God can do His thing.

That does not mean we will be free of calamity. Solomon refers to the reality of misfortune, drenching rain, and falling trees. Obstacles and difficulties and, from a human standpoint, failures and losses may face us. Northern Ireland has had its share of sectarian violence through the years, and a man visiting Belfast was afraid. He hoped to get home safely without being attacked. Suddenly a dark figure jumped out of the shadows and, grabbing him around the neck, stuck the point of a knife against his throat. In a gruff voice the assailant demanded, "Catholic or Protestant?"

Seized with panic, the man reasoned to himself, *If I say Catholic and he's a Protestant—whoosh! If I say Protestant and he's a Catholic, I'm also a goner!* Then he thought of a way out. "I'm a Jew!"

The assailant chuckled, "Ha! I'm the luckiest Arab terrorist in Belfast!"[6]

Sometimes, no matter how hard we try, we lose. Disasters will occur. But that shouldn't keep us back from giving our all, doing our all for the Lord. Nor does it mean presumptuous, thoughtless risk taking! Ecclesiastes 11:2 implies wisdom and carefulness in casting our bread upon the waters. If you asked Philippe Petit if he is a risk taker, he'd say no! "I don't see wire walking as risk taking," he insists. "I have no room in my life for risk. You can't be both a risk taker and a wire walker. I take absolutely no risks. . . . I plan everything the most that I can. I put together with the utmost care that part of my life. I leave nothing up to chance."[7]

When we consider all the careful planning Petit did to walk between the World Trade Center towers—consulting engineers, studying blueprints of the towers, calculating the physics of a taut rope strung between swaying buildings, researching wind velocity—he didn't take risks. He simply did what was possible if ventured the right way.

Solomon doesn't have in mind presumptuous, thoughtless risk taking. Rather he speaks of reaching out to do those things that are morally right, for the sake of truth, in response to God's Word, for God's work, and to meet the needs of people. And then he wants us to do such things with integrity and wisdom as well as with boldness and energy. Whether letting go, pursuing, or expanding, we always do it with wisdom and faith. God's promise is that when we pursue worthy challenges, we will receive the fruit of our labors. "Therefore, my beloved brethren, be steadfast, immovable, always abounding in the work of the Lord, knowing that your toil is not in vain in the Lord" (1 Cor. 15:58). "Let us not lose heart in doing good, for in due time we shall reap if we do not grow weary" (Gal. 6:9).

Instead of protecting ourselves, we need to release ourselves. Escaping the same old rut, we must expand our horizons and experiences and activities. And ceasing to drift along doing the minimum, we should wholeheartedly pursue the opportunities before us. It's time to walk some wires, to see God at work in our lives.

In 1900 British Antarctic explorer Sir Ernest Shackleton placed the following advertisement in London newspapers as he recruited men for the National Antarctic Expedition: "MEN WANTED FOR HAZARDOUS JOURNEY. Small wages, bitter cold, long months of complete darkness, constant danger, safe return doubtful. Honor and recognition in case of success.—Ernest Shackleton."[8]

Who would answer an ad like that? Would you? Evidently many were up to the challenge, because Shackleton received a flood of applicants. "It seemed as though all the men in Great Britain were determined to accompany me," he said later. "The response was overwhelming."[9] Although the expedition failed to reach the South Pole, it was not for lack of able-bodied, ambitious volunteers.

How about it? When was the last time you broke your routine and did something unusual for yourself? for others? for God?

"Get out of your rut!" Solomon declares. Instead of protecting yourself, release yourself to the challenges before you. Get yourself out of that rut and expand your horizons and experiences. Go beyond the minimum and wholeheartedly pursue worthy goals. Don't wait for conditions to be perfect, for things to be free of all risks, but turn your boring life into an exciting and contagious one. Jump into life and experience it! See God work in your life.

---

[1] Ralph Keyes, *Chancing It: Why We Take Risks* (Boston: Little, Brown and Co., 1985), pp. 7-9.

[2] Nadine Stair, "If I Had My Life to Live Over," in Jack Canfield and Mark V. Hansen, eds., *Chicken Soup for the Soul* (Deerfield Beach, Fla.: Health Communications, 1993), pp. 287, 288.

[3] C. Swindoll, *Living on the Ragged Edge,* p. 314.

[4] J. Ellul, *Reason for Being,* p. 226.

[5] *Ibid.*

[6] Swindoll, p. 320.

[7] Keyes, p. 9.

[8] William Bennett, *The Book of Virtues* (New York: Simon and Schuster, 1993), p. 493.

[9] *Ibid.*

18

TEDDY BEARS, LOLLIPOPS, AND OLYMPIC GOLD

Rejoice, young man, during your childhood,
*   and let your heart be pleasant during the days*
*   of young manhood.*
And follow the impulses of your heart and the desires of your eyes.
Yet know that God will bring you to judgment for all these things.
So, remove vexation from your heart
*   and put away pain from your body,*
*   because childhood and the prime of life are fleeting.*
Remember also your Creator in the days of your youth,
*   before the evil days come and the years draw near*
*   when you will say,*
*   "I have no delight in them."*

*   —Ecclesiastes 11:9-12:1*

When 18-year-old Kerri Strug "stuck" her landing, she saved the gold for the U.S.A. and earned her place in Olympic history. The 1996 women's gymnastic team had barely made it through the compulsories. They weren't at their best in the freestyle, either. But the other women's teams were making mistakes too. By the last rotation the U.S. women had edged within reach of the gold. However, after watching teammate Dominique Moceanu fall twice on her vaults, Strug knew she needed to land one of her two

179

attempts to assure the U.S. a victory. But on her first attempt Strug not only fell—she severely twisted her left ankle. She literally limped her way back to vault again, repeatedly shaking her injured ankle along the way. The more than 32,000 Georgia Dome fans, her coach, Bela Karolyi, her parents and teammates, the Russian team, and millions of viewers worldwide watched and wondered.

No one knew how much pain she was in. Only Kerri knew. But she wasn't thinking about the pain. "I knew that the gold medal was kind of slipping away from us and all the hard work we had all done over the years was falling apart in just a few seconds," she said later. Faced with cleanly performing the same vault with a severely sprained ankle, she grit her teeth and ran. Her vault was high, seemingly effortless, and precise. And she nailed her landing—with one foot. It was incredible, now that we know the extent of her injury. But Kerri did it! She got the gold for her team and put her name in Olympic history. Her score of 9.712 was enough to give the U.S. a team total of 389.225, beating the Russians by a mere 0.821.[1]

As she stood on one leg at the award ceremony while receiving her gold medal, and as coach Bela Karolyi carried her away in his big arms, Kerri's face said volumes—so young-looking, yet having accomplished so much. For the most part, the faces around the 1996 Olympic Village were young faces. Some were the faces of mere children. NBC news commentators even referred to a bunch of the U.S. women athletes as the "Lollipop Gang." They were teenage girls with a vision for gold, including 14-year-old Dominique Moceanu, 14-year-old Amanda Beard with her favorite teddy bear, 15-year-old Beth Botsford, and 16-year-old queen of distance swimming, Brooke Bennet.

The one-two that the U.S. did in the women's 100-meter backstroke highlights the impact such youthfulness expressed in the 1996 Summer Olympics. Twenty-five-year-old Whitney Hedgepath got the silver. But 15-year-old Beth Botsford received the gold. That little 15-year-old beat the 25-year-old by a full minute and 1.19 hundredths of a second.

It brings Solomon's words to life: "Remember also your Creator in the days of your youth, before the evil days come and the years draw near when you will say, 'I have no delight in them'" (Eccl. 12:1). When I think of the vitality, the energy, the passion, the vision, and the potential of youth, I think of these words and all those wasted years in Solomon's own life. When he was in his prime he loved the Lord with a passion. Somehow he got distracted. *How can I make my mark in the world?* he no doubt wondered. *How can I achieve success? How can I find love? Or know happiness?* Solomon had been everywhere, done everything, and followed every dream to which a person could aspire *under the sun.* He played the world's game and lost. *What good came of my life?* he wondered as he looked back on those vibrant moments when he was young, when his face was glorious with triumph and promise and life, when he had so much to give God.

When Your Face Is Glorious

Looking back, Solomon gives us three bits of advice: Rejoice! Remove! Remember!

"Rejoice, young man, during your childhood, and let your heart be pleasant during the days of young manhood" (Eccl. 11:9).

A story tells about identical twins, one of which was a hopeless optimist. "Everything is coming up roses!" he would say. The other was a sad and hopeless pessimist who viewed everything and anything in an impossible and objectionable light. The worried parents of the boys took them to a psychologist for help.

He suggested a plan to the parents to balance the twins' personalities. "On their next birthday, put them in separate rooms to open their gifts. Give the pessimist the best toys you can afford, and give the optimist a box of manure." The parents followed the instructions and carefully observed the results.

When they peeked in on the pessimist, they heard him audibly complaining, "I don't like the color of this computer. . . . I'll bet this

181

calculator will break. . . . I don't like this game. . . . I know someone who's got a bigger toy car than this. . . ."

Tiptoeing across the corridor, the parents saw their little optimist gleefully throwing the manure up in the air, giggling to himself. "You can't fool me! Where there's this much manure, there's gotta be a pony!"[2]

"Rejoice, young man, during your childhood, and let your heart be pleasant during the days of young manhood." In other words, don't hang around with an attitude. Get a life! Let your heart be optimistic and filled with promise. Look on the bright side of things. Be positive and celebrate. The form of the Hebrew word translated "pleasant" suggests a conscious decision to "let your heart delight you." It sees inner gladness and joy as a choice. Whenever I ask my youngest son what he has been doing all day, he says, "Playing." I get the same answer every day! He never gets tired of playing. Nor should our hearts ever tire of finding pleasure in life or seeing the promise of gladness and innocent joy.

Rejoice has its balance in remove. "Remove vexation from your heart and put away pain from your body, because childhood and the prime of life are fleeting" (verse 10). The Hebrew word translated "vexation" or "anxiety" means to agitate, stir up, or provoke the heart to a heated condition that in turn leads to specific actions. It combines ideas of anger and resentment. When such emotions exist in a person's life, it leads to rebellion and a spirit of independence. In other words, Scripture warns us to rid ourselves of a rebellious spirit that creates anger, exasperation, and bitterness at others or at what life appears to dole out to us.

On top of that, we must remove the things that will destroy us or bring evil to us. "Put away pain from your body." We need to get rid of those things that produce pain—the things that leave us spiritually empty, morally jaded, mentally weak, and physically wasted. Evil or moral compromise in any form will always pay dreadful dividends. It will lead to scars, heartaches, and regrets that we will carry long into our old age. Sorrow and guilt have a way of stealing our peace and joy. We can genuinely rejoice only when we remove such pain givers.

Finally, Solomon writes that we need to remember. "Remember also your Creator in the days of your youth." Having reviewed all the possibilities that life offers, he challenges us to serve our Creator with a passion while we still have a future and purpose in our lives. During your youth, when you are at the peak of your strength and glory, remember you have a Creator. While you are in your glory, turn your glorious face toward the one who created you![3]

You know what I think Solomon is saying? "Remember your Creator when all possibilities lie open before you and you can offer all your strength intact for His service." The time to remember is not after you become senile and paralyzed, ready to check out! Or when you are bored with life, or filled with sorrows and guilt, or afraid of what lies ahead. At such moments it may not be too late to find forgiveness and salvation, but it is too late to serve God with your whole heart and mind and the best of your gifts and with all your potential. We need to turn to God before the time comes when we say, "I have no pleasure in them" (Eccl. 12:1, NKJV). We are to remember God in our youth so that we can offer Him a face radiant with joy. Only then will our prayer be a glorious giving of thanks, not a sterile lament!

The days of trouble, the failure of bodily and mental strength, and the lack of pleasure in the pursuits of life are not the occasions to begin to think of a godly lifestyle in this world or of our need of God. That's Solomon's point in the first seven verses of chapter 12. Here he presents graphic imagery of aging with its mental dullness and depression, physical ailments and limitations. We have nothing left to offer God then except existential angst.

I was on a gymnastic team during my high school and college days. The horizontal bar was my specialty, but I also did routines on the parallel bars. Both demanded a lot of strength and agility. I was in pretty good shape during those years. Strength, endurance, and rhythm—I had it. Full giant swings on the horizontal bar were always a thrill, demanding timing and a vicelike grip. That was years ago. The last time I tried a handstand I got dizzy. I figure I might make it through one complete giant swing, but I expect the centrifugal force in such a move would now pull me away, hurling me horizontally through the air and landing me somewhere on my back 40 or so feet away. I no longer have the edge I had in those years. Even then I was not really up to a gymnast's full potential. Actually I started gymnastics too late in life. I was 16 at the time. By then my muscles had already set, so to speak. They were just too tight. Certain moves, such as dislocates, were almost impossible and quite painful for me to do. I just wasn't limber enough. Had I started at 9 or 10, it would have made all the difference. My potential would have been increased proportionally.

We must choose earlier in our life. There is a time when choices are really possible, and then comes the time when we no longer have any real choices. Up against a wall, we find ourselves obliged to obey or pray or reach out to God by necessity. Then pain is so deep or our time is so short.

I believe the message here includes most of us—whatever our age—whose face is glorious with good things in life. Now, now while we have life and something we still call good in life, we must give ourselves wholeheartedly to the living God of heaven. We must prepare not just for eternity, but to act decisively for the living God now.

18 Holes in Your Mind

Major James Nesmeth loved golf and dreamed of improving his game. He succeeded in developing a unique method of achieving his goal. Until he devised it, though, he was just your average weekend golfer, shooting in the mid to low 90s. Then, for seven years, he completely quit the game, never touching a club or setting foot on a fairway. Ironically, it was during this seven-year break from the game that Nesmeth came up with his amazingly effective technique for improving his game. In fact, the first time he set foot on a golf course after his seven-year hiatus he shot an astonishing 74. He had cut 20 strokes off his average without having swung a club in seven years. What was his secret? It was "visualization."

Nesmeth spent that seven-year hiatus in a North Vietnamese prisoner of war camp. For those seven years he lived in a four-and-one-half-foot-high and five-foot-long cage. During that time he saw no one, talked to no one, and experienced no physical activity. Realizing that he had to find some way to occupy his mind or he would lose his sanity and probably his life, Nesmeth learned to visualize. In his mind he selected his favorite golf course and started playing golf. Every day he played a full 18 holes at the imaginary country club of his dreams. He experienced everything to the last detail. What style and color clothes he would wear. The shoes he would choose. The distinct fragrances of the flowers along the way and the scent of freshly trimmed grass. The weather conditions. Every detail of the tee, including individual blades of grass, the surrounding trees, the singing birds, the grip of the clubs in his hands, the ball arcing down the exact center of the fairway. He visualized it all.

In the real world he had no reason to hurry or place to go. So in his mind he took every step on his way to the ball just as if he were physically on the course. It required just as long in imaginary time to play 18 holes as it would have taken in reality. He didn't omit a detail. Not once did he ever miss a shot, hook, or slice.

Seven days a week. Four hours a day. Eighteen holes. Seven years. It cut 20 strokes off his game.[4]

"Remember also your Creator," Solomon says. All God asks is that we grant Him a place in our present memory. Instead of leaving Him in an old unused place—like some image covered with dust—let God have a significant spot in our thinking. He does not impose Himself on us. Instead, He is, as Jacques Ellul phrases it, "utterly discreet." We can forget Him, cast Him aside, fail to concern ourself with Him. If we wish, He remains hidden and patient in the shadows of our lives. God remains in a silence broken only by a call from someone who speaks in His name—who takes the time to bring Him into their conscious present thinking. Remembering is active! When we remember, we act and do something.

During NBC's coverage of the 1996 Atlanta Summer Olympics I heard one of the members from the Unified Men's Gymnastic Team say something incredible about his coach, Leoanive Arkiave. "He's like god to me. In my world I would be nothing if it weren't for him." And so with our Creator God. All our happiness, all our blessings, everything we call good in our life comes from Him. He is the Father of lights through whom every good thing is bestowed and every perfect gift is given (James 1:17). We are to remember all He has done for us, remember that He is there, and in our heart of hearts exclaim, "In my world I would be nothing if it weren't for Him!"

Rejoice! Remove! Remember! When you do, you can then safely "follow," as Solomon says, "the impulses of your heart and the desires of your eyes" (Eccl. 11:9). It's the only safe way. When God is a part of your life, your thinking, the passion of your heart, your impulses and desires will always be for Him—morally right, spiritually genuine, eternally true.

While you are in your glory, turn your glorious face toward the One who created you!

---

[1] Rany Kennedy, "Injured Gymnast Vaults Into History," *The Herald-Palladium,* July 24, 1996.

[2] "The Optimist," in J. Canfield and M. V. Hansen, eds., *A Second Helping of Chicken Soup for the Soul,* p. 180.

[3] J. Ellul, *Reason for Being,* pp. 280-282.

[4] "18 Holes in His Mind," *A Second Helping of Chicken Soup for the Soul,* p. 235.

A LAST NAIL
FOR THE LAST DAY

"Vanities of vanities," says the Preacher, "all is vanity."
In addition to being a wise man,
    the Preacher also taught the people knowledge;
    and he pondered, searched out and arranged many proverbs.
The Preacher sought to find delightful words
    and to write words of truth correctly.
The words of wise men are like goads,
    and masters of these collections are like well-driven nails;
    they are given by one Shepherd.
But beyond this, my son, be warned:
    the writing of many books is endless,
    and excessive devotion to books is wearying to the body.
The conclusion, when all has been heard, is:
    fear God and keep His commandments,
    because this applies to every person.
For God will bring every act to judgment,
    everything which is hidden,
    whether it is good or evil.

                                 —Ecclesiastes 12:8-14

I stepped into Barnes and Noble to find some good books on Montana. My family was headed for the Big Sky State for some backpacking and mountain biking adventure, so I wanted to plan ahead. It would be no casual browse, though, as I had an appointment to make. But as I hurried down the main aisle, my pace slackened. There along the way were stacks and tables of the latest and best-sellers. Books just seemed to jump out at me from every direction. It was as if every book within sight whispered, "Read me! Read me!" The ones with the slick, colorfully designed jackets and captivating titles teased the loudest. "Go ahead. Pick me up. Take a look inside. See what I have to offer." I found myself stopping here and there to admire the artistic covers, note some titles, and scan a few flaps. Since I'm always on the lookout for sermon titles, illustrations, or the latest things people are thinking about, I indulged myself with several titles along the way. When I finally reached the travel section, I ended up inspecting books on more states than Montana. One or two from Europe found themselves in my hand as well. Naturally, I was late to my appointment!

Authors who really want their books read will make sure they catch your attention, stir your interest, and lock into your imagination.

Have you noticed how many books include perceptive selling points on their covers? How they announce the great benefit you will receive if you buy and read them? Consider Jack Canfield and Mark Hansen's *Aladdin Factor*.[1] Under the cover title you find a bright red-lettered paragraph set against a stark white background. "One of the greatest lessons you'll ever learn is how to ask for what you want. Canfield and Hansen show you how."[2] Or Stephen Covey's *The Seven Habits of Highly Effective People*.[3] "Powerful Lessons in Personal Change," it announces. "Destined to be *the* personal leadership handbook of the decade." Charles Swindoll's *Hope Again*[4] uses the same purposeful strategy. "Hope again when life hurts and dreams fade." "Find Hope to press on . . . Hope to endure . . . Hope to stay focused . . . Hope to see dreams fulfilled . . ." Who of us could look past that cover without a heart tug and at least thumbing through the table of contents? Hope is in high demand in our postmodern world.

Readers apparently want to know the basics. "What will this

book do for me? Why should I buy it? Why should I read it?" Sleek and clever jackets scratch where people itch. They touch their souls, their pain, their yearnings, their dreams, teasing with well-phrased questions, novel-sounding solutions, and brazen promises to meet some particular need better than any rival book.

Solomon was no different. His opening salvo and parting shot are typical marketing—"Read my book!" Now, he doesn't say it in those words, but his meaning is the same. Few can read his haunting bookend assertion "Meaningless! Meaningless! . . . Everything is meaningless!" (Eccl. 1:2; 12:8, NIV) without some gut reaction—either agreeing fully with its existential angst, hoping against hope that it is not so, or assuming that there's some riddle or paradox here that opens the way to real meaning. First page, last page—"Meaningless! Meaningless! . . . Everything is meaningless!" Surely our restless postmodern world, our MTV-driven latchkey, Generation X would concur! Here's a line that raises a nod! It speaks my language.

Solomon doesn't leave us guessing as to what his collection of pithy sayings will do for us either: "The words of the wise men are like goads," he writes, "and masters of these collections are like well-driven nails; they are given by one Shepherd" (Eccl. 12:11). Same purposeful strategy, selling points, and evocative promise.

You know what goads are? My thesaurus lists such words as prompt, poke, pester, needle, motivate, irritate, stimulate, spur, arouse, impel, catalyst, and more. A goad is something that prods into action and increases speed. For example, a cattle prod. In Solomon's time goads were big long sharp sticks, possibly with iron points. Cattle herders would jab them against the hindquarters of the tough-skinned beasts to move them along. Today we have electric cattle prods that deliver high-voltage shocks. They work quite well! When I was a boy working for a cattle rancher, the foreman slipped a cattle prod under the covers of a dude who had overslept. He awakened *reeeeaal* fast. We laughed all day on that one.

I heard a CBS newscast announce how some transit officials in India used electric cattle prods to move passengers along at a crowded train stop. The people didn't like that kind of tactic, so they rioted for several days afterward. Goads are prodders, something to catch our attention, get us going, quicken our pace.

And well-driven nails? Nails secure things so they don't move or blow away or change easily. Take a well-driven stake that keeps a tent in place, securing it to the ground. Have you ever seen what happens to a tent that wasn't staked down well when a high wind came? One of the lingering images in my mind is the very first back-pack trip I took my young wife on. We had climbed Mount Marcy in New York and pitched our tent on a ridge that opened toward the valley below. It was a great view.

Behind and to the sides were rich green pines and white birch. All around were gorgeous mountains. The sun was shining, and a gentle breeze ascended from the valley. It was a great day. But as the sun set behind us, we noticed an eerie dark cloud looming down in the valley below. Soon that gentle breeze was a gusting, howling wind. Within moments a roaring darkness engulfed our little tent. For the next couple hours I wondered when the stakes would pull and we would be literally "gone with the wind." But I had driven the nails well. They held secure. Not a single stake pulled out during that night of storm. In spite of all the noise and wind outside, we were safe—much to my wife's relief.

Words are like cattle prods and tent spikes. They can motivate us to action and they can rivet particular thoughts in our mind. "I'm writing words that will prod people to action," Solomon tells us. "I'm writing words that will nail things down, securing them in place. Motivation and dead-on truth! That's what you'll find in this collection of proverbs and pithy sayings. If you're struggling with the meaning of life, if you think everything is meaningless, I've got what you need. In fact, the meaning of life just might surprise you."

The skeptic David Hume was seen walking in the snow long before daybreak one frigid morning. He, along with others, was making his way to a little chapel in which George Whitefield was preaching. Someone who knew Hume said, "I didn't know you believed this kind of stuff."

"I don't," he responded, "but that man in the chapel does, and I can't stay away."

Something about words can goad even skeptics. They can't silence the words, because they are prodding at them, exploding silently in their minds.[5] And it's even more so when it is truth that is so compelling—truth nailed down as something sure and trustworthy.

Now listen to the context in which Solomon sets his imagery of goads and well-driven nails: he "sought to find delightful words and to write words of truth correctly" (Eccl. 12:10). The Hebrew for the word "delightful" means "that in which one takes delight." Delightful words are winsome words, words easy to grasp and readily applied to life. "Hey," Solomon declares, "I searched for words that would win a hearing. Expressions that would clarify and grab the reader's attention. I wanted the words I chose to rivet themselves into minds cluttered with a lot of other things, so that my book wouldn't just pass by unnoticed." As J. B. Phillips once said: "If words are to enter men's hearts and bear fruit, they must be the right words shaped cunningly to pass men's defenses and explode silently and effectually within their minds."[6]

Who likes to hear about underwear? Sounds embarrassing or boring, doesn't it? But anyone watching the Atlanta Summer Olympics found themselves being "briefed" on the subject by Michael Jordan. No one will ever forget the comical Hanes underwear commercial about the ancient Olympians who competed naked. Creative imagery ingeniously focused on a specific event— the Olympics. It got your attention, nailed down the idea, and made you laugh. Most important of all to the sponsor, it made you think about Hanes. Hopefully it goaded you into buying the purple briefs or the red boxers Jordan had used to cover the naked statues of ancient Olympic competitors. I'm sure Hanes would have been glad if you had bought plain old white briefs, too.

My boys got a kick out of the Tabasco commercial that premiered during Super Bowl XXXII. They'll never forget the rednecked guy sitting on his front-porch rocking chair eating thick-crust pizza. Several empty jars of hot Tabasco lay strewn on the porch by his feet. Beads of sweat hung on his rotund face as if he'd just come in from the rain. He had a sun-burned blush about him and a crazed stare in his eyes. Above the crunch of a mouthful of pizza crust one heard the high whine of a mosquito. The guy took his gaze off the pizza and watched the mosquito land on his bare leg and then pierce through the skin. The mosquito soon filled and flew off. About 10 feet away—*boom!* It exploded as if hit by a heat-sinking missile. Too much Tabasco for that guy. Now when my sons see a bottle of Tabasco, they see a mosquito exploding in midair. Another idea creatively nailed down.

Now imagine Ecclesiastes—Solomon's well-crafted words, God's Word!—like Tabasco sauce couched in what outwardly appears to satisfy hungry souls. Someone comes in for a drink of something they think they want, and as they go away, *boom!*—something explodes in their head, in their conscience. They've suddenly seen truth. Suddenly had some new moral insight and abruptly met God in a new and unexpected way.

Solomon worked hard to find living words, practical words, picturesque words with which to present deep eternal truth. As a pastor (he calls himself "the Preacher"), Solomon sought out the right words and methods of delivery so that God's Word would penetrate lives clearly, practically, and powerfully. Let's review a few: "Vanity of vanities! All is vanity" (Eccl. 1:2); "I hated life" (Eccl. 2:17); "I congratulated the dead who are already dead more than the living who are still living" (Eccl. 4:2); "One tenth of one percent of the men I interviewed could be said to be wise, but not one woman!" (Eccl. 7:28, TLB); "There is an appointed time for everything. And there is a time for every event under heaven" (Eccl. 3:1); "The day of one's death is better than the day of one's birth" (Eccl. 7:1); "The fate of the sons of men and the fate of beasts is the same" (Eccl. 3:19); "A live dog is better than a dead lion" (Eccl. 9:4). What imagery. What a book. Hot Tabasco!

As I read these words—"the Preacher sought to find delightful words and to write words of truth correctly"—I can't help thinking of the challenge we have in keeping proper balance between relevance and truth. Can something be both true and irrelevant? Can something be both untrue and relevant? Of course! Most people today aren't looking for truth; they are looking for relief, for hope, for meaning, and for happiness. Their existential angst causes them to plug into whatever appears to relieve their pain or solve their problems. Most people in our postmodern world find the Bible irrelevant. They would regard church and worship and Christian lifestyle meaningless as well. And yet Scripture is filled with incredibly relevant truth. Our challenge is to *show* the Bible's pertinence by applying its message to human lives. To be both incredibly truthful and incredibly relevant. When we share biblical principles in a way that meets a need, it creates a hunger for more truth. Being genuinely relevant produces a genuine interest in truth.

For Adventists as they advance into the twenty-first century I believe Ecclesiastes provides a provocative example of creatively packaged words rich in imagery and gripping relevance, but words of truth crafted correctly and with integrity. We need to find the right mix of apt, motivating, gripping, attractive, packaged, but nailed-down and uncompromising, candid, present truth. Each of us must present honest truth for this final generation, but we must do it in a winsome way easily grasped and readily applied to life. Connecting with people, we must build bridges between where they are in their thinking and what they need in the mind of God. Ecclesiastes points the way as an ancient, 3,000-year-old book directs those searching for hope in a postmodern world struggling for meaning. As a people we need to blow the dust off Ecclesiastes.

We must never fear being relevant; we must fear that in our desire for relevance we will somehow not handle truth correctly. That in the process of being meaningful we in no way compromise truth. Remember, we cannot *make* the Bible relevant—it *already is*. Rather, we are to *show* its relevance by applying its message personally to our lives. Our ability to set forth the truths of God's Word correctly is in proportion to how much we ourselves understand through personal experience just how relevant the Bible really is.

If you were reading a sleek colored book jacket for Ecclesiastes and asked yourself, "What will this book do for me?" you'd find Solomon saying, "It will give you goads and nails. Motivation and dead-on truth set in a creative, riveting wrap. Honest truth that's hard to miss and hard to turn away from! Truth given by a *Shepherd* who understands and cares [see Eccl. 12:11]. Furthermore, to continue searching for meaning after you've read my book is foolhardy. An endless quest, it will wear down even your body. What I've written says it all, says it right, and says enough!" If only we would believe him.

Life's Bottom Line

"Why do I need the goads and nails?" some potential reader might ask. "Why do I need to be motivated or have truth nailed down tight in my thinking?" Solomon brings it down to life's bottom line. "The conclusion, when all has been heard, is: fear God and keep His commandments, because this applies to every person. For God will bring every act to judgment, everything which is hidden, whether it is good or evil" (Eccl. 12:13, 14).

Why do I need to be spiritually and morally motivated and have truth nailed down tight in my thinking? Why does truth need to come to me in a provocative new way that explodes in my imagination? Because God is real! He is not just some abstract, distant benign being or mere universal knowledge, as our modern world implies. No! God is one who speaks and commands. His commandments express universal truths that apply to every man and woman.

We need to take God seriously, enter into relationship with Him, and do what He says.

Why do I need to take God seriously and do what He commands? Because the living God takes us seriously—our words, our thoughts, our actions, even the hidden things. Ecclesiastes announces that meaning exists beyond the moment. Life lived *under the sun* has *above the sun* significance. That day of judgment on history's horizon affirms that our world is headed toward a goal. We live in a moral universe in which we are significant and accountable—we're more than beasts. Our world plunges toward a compelling juristic reckoning. In the final analysis, we'll all do business with the living Creator God. Our lives will replay themselves and we will be held accountable for what we did. Ecclesiastes announces that how we live now—every moment and every thing—has tremendous consequence.

I am continually amazed at the instant replays during sports events. Who really touched the line first? Was that foot out-of-bounds? The cameras back up, slow down, stop, magnify. Trained eyes then see the facts. The refs can call it only one way. I'm amazed, too, how the FBI and other law-enforcement agencies piece their way through criminal and terrorist cases. Evidence at times can be so minuscule and yet so profoundly indisputable in what conclusions it declares. In that epochal moment Solomon calls judgment, each one of us will give an account of the life we have lived *under the sun*. Everything will be replayed, carefully examined, shown for what it really was and what it really means about our character, our values, our choices, and the place God truly holds in our hearts.

So Ecclesiastes is a timely book with a timely message, one reaching down to our this-is-all-there-is generation. The focus of God's appeal has not changed through the centuries. "Fear God, and give Him glory, because the hour of His judgment has come," cries the first angel of Revelation 14 (verse 7). Judgment is a truth that none of us living in this last restless generation of ours dare take lightly. None of us can reduce it to mere historic Adventism, somehow no longer relevant or graceless. Unless we come to grips with the message of Ecclesiastes, we will not come through judgment with a positive verdict. We will not make the kingdom of heaven. Ecclesiastes raises questions about our values and priorities. Where are we searching for meaning and happiness: money? education? pleasure? things? sex? How are we doing in our relationships? What kind of dead flies are floating in our tea? What kind of reputation do we have in the world? What kind of skeletons lurk in our closet? Where is God in our affections?

Romans declares that "there is therefore now no condemnation for those who are in Christ Jesus" (Rom. 8:1). Daniel assures that judgment will be "passed in favor" of those who know and love God (Dan. 7:22). Is it not now the time to remember God? to fear Him? to listen to His voice? to hide our lives in His grace? to wash our robes and make them white in the blood of the Lamb? to love God with all our heart and soul and mind?

Solomon's well-driven nails—honest truth for a final generation—concludes on a high note, because the Person of God is real, and we need to reflect His righteousness *under the sun*. We need to find God, and to know God is *real life*. As Augustine said: "He who has God has everything. He who does not have God has nothing. He who has God and everything has no more than he who has God and nothing."

Before the Unthinkable

Olympic springboard diver Mark Lenzi went to Barcelona wondering what Olympic gold could get for him. He was in search of money, fame, contracts. Although he got gold, he also learned first-hand the fleeting euphoria such *under the sun* experience brings. Fifteen minutes on the victors' stand before cheering crowds, bright lights, and flashing cameras. That's it! Lenzi went into post-Olympic depression, gaining weight, going out of control in his moral life until he crashed. Life became the pits—until Coach Billingsley found him, affirmed him, and psyched him back up for Atlanta. Would that last any longer?

A few minutes of fame and glory with the gold here? Or eternity? Meaningless life in an absurd world? Or meaningful relationship with a caring God? Which would you have? Nothing here really lasts. Only God endures.

"We're just fragile candles flickering in the wind," Elton John suggests. "A *Titanic* generation," warns James Cameron. Today we're a generation haunted with the unthinkable. In the midst of that piercing angst the living God of heaven calls our weary hearts to Himself before the unthinkable happens. Before it is too late.

Life is meant to be a lifelong love affair with the living God, who dwells *above the sun*. That vision of life includes you.

---

[1] Jack Canfield and Mark Victor Hansen, *The Aladdin Factor* (New York: Berkley Books, 1995).

[2] *Ibid.*

[3] Steven R. Covey, *The Seven Habits of Highly Effective People* (New York: Simon and Schuster, 1989).

[4] Charles R. Swindoll, *Hope Again* (Dallas: Word Publishing, 1996).

[5] ———, *Living on the Ragged Edge,* p. 370.

[6] J. B. Phillips, as quoted in Swindoll, *Living on the Ragged Edge,* p. 368.

READ THIS BOOK
AGAIN AND AGAIN

When Solomon built the Temple in Jerusalem, he decided to dedicate it at the season of the Feast of Sukkot (1 Kings 8). Sukkot, usually translated as Tabernacles or Feast of Booths, occurred for seven days, lasting from Tishri 15 to 21. It was the third pilgrimage festival that God called His people to celebrate together in His presence (Ex. 23:14-17). "In biblical times, Sukkot was the most important festival of all; in fact, it was referred to simply as *ha-hag*—'the festival' (e.g., 1 Kings 12:32)."[1] It was a grand harvesttime of rejoicing and celebration, feasting, music, and impressive ceremonies, including the water-drawing ceremony and the willow waving.

The most important ritual of Sukkot (hence its name) was living in a *sukkah*. A *sukkah* is a little hut or temporary shelter made from wood or canvas and covered with branches of trees and plants in such a manner as to ensure enough shade from the sun, but not so much as to prevent one from seeing the stars at night.[2] "You shall live in booths *[sukkot]* for seven days; all the native-born in Israel shall live in booths *[sukkot],* so that your generations may know that I had the sons of Israel live in booths *[sukkot]* when I brought them out of the land of Egypt. I am the Lord your God" (Lev. 23:39-43).

The *sukkah* (plural *sukkot)* had to be a temporary structure, not a permanent one. God intended it to remind the Israelites of the portability of their huts or tents in the desert as they wandered from place to place for 40 years. A paradigm of their journey,[3] it would

198

stress one of the themes of the holiday—the impermanence of human life.[4] In essence, each Jewish family would treat the *sukkah* as their home during the holiday. There they would eat their meals and celebrate God's earthly blessings of life. And there they would lie down in the darkness to sleep through the night. In so doing they would reenact their journey to liberation—from Egypt to the Promised Land. Thus Sukkot paid tribute to Israel's journey in a desert while celebrating the produce of the land of Israel. Sukkot affirmed the holiness of pleasure, even while it infused pleasure in the holy. The festival celebrated material wealth even as it warned that it is "vanity of vanities."[5]

We can only speculate why Solomon chose Sukkot as the time to dedicate the Temple. Possibly it was simply the first pilgrim festival when all Israel would come up to Jerusalem after the builders had completed it. But perhaps he also saw some analogy between the fragile *sukkah*—open to the sky, to wind, to wanderer—and the house that he knew could not contain the God of earth and heaven.[6] "But will God indeed dwell on the earth?" he prayed. "Behold, heaven and the highest heaven cannot contain Thee, how much this house which I have built!" (1 Kings 8:27). Perhaps Solomon was saying that the Temple in all its grandeur was also but a fragile *sukkah*.[7]

What a commentary on life! No wonder that in the course of time Ecclesiastes became one of the main readings during the days of the Feast of Sukkot.[8] As Solomon's firsthand commentary on the fragility of human life and the vanity of everything that people possess and experience in life, Ecclesiastes and Sukkot fit. "In this festival of fragility and the precariousness of human shelter, Israel understood that only God protected her. All security, all solid foundations, were called into question once a year."[9] What better book to read during this time than Ecclesiastes? It says it all. All the ironic and paradoxical themes we have touched on in Ecclesiastes resonated with Israel's weeklong enacted drama of living in their ridiculous and fragile shelters under the stars, in order to shelter life and joy in life—all the while celebrating earthly life and tasting its sen-

199

sory blessings. Both Sukkot and Ecclesiastes proclaim human existence as essentially self-contradictory. Each reminds us that we should accept vulnerability and live more deeply.[10] In light of the essential link that has been drawn between Ecclesiastes and Sukkot, Ellul writes: "What book speaks more eloquently of this fragility, challenges everything, requires us to examine our conscience, sweeps away all our rock-solid certainties? It leaves us alone with our precarious destiny, stripped bare to experience the only genuine security: the security offered by the sovereign Master of history."[11]

Imagine, every year living in a *sukkah* for a week and reading, of all things, Ecclesiastes. Israel had that kind of experience built into her yearly spiritual journey. Every year. Same time. Same fragile shelter. Same script. They couldn't go through the year without listening to Ecclesiastes. It was the message they would need to hear till Messiah would appear and the promised new age became reality.

How about you and me? How often do we need to hear the perturbing, unconventional but hope-filled, down-to-earth message of Ecclesiastes? When was the last time you read Ecclesiastes? Did you take the time to read it through while wending your way through these pages of mine? Or did you just stay with my thoughts? Will you even now go on to read the whole of Ecclesiastes for yourself?

I suspect Ecclesiastes may be for us one of those obscure biblical books that we hardly read, if at all. When we do pick up Ecclesiastes, it's usually read as part of our journey through the Bible. A necessary stop along the way. You know—we've just been thoroughly moved by the Psalms that seem to speak so eloquently to us. Then we kind of hop and skip our way through Proverbs, hoping to catch a one-liner here or there that we can hang on to (all the while wondering how all those pithy statements relate to each other and if we will manage to stay awake). Then we hit Ecclesiastes! We're not sure what to do with it. Our brains get tired trying to figure it out. Once again we move along to easier, more inspirational things.

Most of us remember Ecclesiastes only for its support of our position on the state of the dead ("the living know that they shall die:

but the dead know not any thing" [9:5]), the need to consider our Creator in the days of our youth, that there's a time for everything under the sun, and that maybe God makes everything beautiful in His time. Beyond that? Ecclesiastes would hardly fare as one of our favorites. It's not the kind of book that warrants our reading every year. Nor is it a trusted friend who says it like it is and somehow really knows what's going on deep inside us.

We reread few books unless their message resonates with our experience in life so much that they continue to stir our imagination in a way that draws us back for more. When that happens, each reading becomes a new journey. We find things we missed earlier. Then we linger on thoughts that speak powerfully to our hearts or give us the perspective we need to go on. Such a book is a friend who speaks to us and for us. Sukkot provided that kind of recurring moment with Ecclesiastes. Because they heard it again and again, Ecclesiastes touched the existential core of Israel's very experience. Israel heard it often enough to become familiar with its imagery and find both instruction and joy in its message.

We have no such tradition that will bring us again and again to Ecclesiastes. Nothing built into our yearly spiritual journey reminds us that all of life is lived in a *sukkah* and that we must read Ecclesiastes in order to put it all together. That's why I want to challenge you just now to create your own annual pilgrimage to Ecclesiastes. To read it repeatedly until its imagery becomes familiar to you. Until you, too, find both instruction and joy in its message. In the process, maybe—just maybe—you'll pick this book up again. I hope so.

During Sukkot Jesus extended one of His most marvelous invitations. It was the last day of the festival. By this time the people were wearied from the long season of festivity. All week long they had engaged in a continual scene of pomp and festivity. They had eaten and slept in their *sukkah*. Light and color had dazzled their eyes, and the richest music had regaled their ears. They had waved the willow branches, and had shouted gladly from their *sukkah* in answer to the

201

shrill blast of silver trumpets as the priests dipped a golden flagon into the Kedron brook as part of the impressive water-drawing ceremony. Ecclesiastes, too, had been read. They knew the script well. Suddenly Jesus lifted up His voice, in deep passionate tones that rang through the courts of the Temple: "If any man is thirsty, let him come to Me and drink. He who believes in Me, as the Scripture said, 'From his innermost being shall flow rivers of living water'" (John 7:38). They were thirsting amidst thanksgiving. "There had been nothing in all this round of ceremonies to meet the wants of the spirit, nothing to satisfy the thirst of the soul for that which perishes not. Jesus had invited them to come and drink of the fountain of life, of that which would be in them a well of water, springing up unto eternal life." [12]

"Jesus knew the wants of the soul. Pomp, riches, and honor cannot satisfy the heart. 'If any man thirst, let him come unto Me.' The rich, the poor, the high, the low, are alike welcome. He promises to relieve the burdened mind, to comfort the sorrowing, and to give hope to the despondent. Many of those who heard Jesus were mourners over disappointed hopes, many were nourishing a secret grief, many were seeking to satisfy their restless longing with the things of the world and the praise of men; but when all was gained, they found that they had toiled only to reach a broken cistern, from which they could not quench their thirst. Amid the glitter of the joyous scene they stood, dissatisfied and sad. That sudden cry, 'If any man thirst,' startled them from their sorrowful meditation, and as they listened to the words that followed, their minds kindled with a new hope. The Holy Spirit presented the symbol before them until they saw in it the offer of the priceless gift of salvation." [13]

Such is the heartfelt appeal of Ecclesiastes. Read it again and again and again until you hear the voice of Jesus calling you to Himself, giving you meaning, hope, and life. Until you find contentment in a disappointing world.

---

[1] Michael Strassfeld, *The Jewish Holidays: A Guide and Commentary* (New York: Harper and Row, Publishers, 1985), p. 126.

[2] *Ibid.,* pp. 125-127; Hyman E. Goldin, *A Treasury of Jewish Holidays* (New York: Twayne Publishers, 1952), p. 42.

[3] Irving Greenberg, *The Jewish Way: Living the Holidays* (New York: Summit Books, 1988), p. 105.

[4] Strassfeld, p. 127.

[5] Greenberg, pp. 98, 99.

[6] Arthur I. Waskow, *Seasons of Our Joy: A Handbook of Jewish Festivals* (New York: Bantam Books, 1982), p. 49.

[7] *Ibid.,* p. 50.

[8] Strassfeld, pp. 126, 134, 135, 139; Ellul, pp. 42-46.

[9] Ellul, p. 45.

[10] Greenberg, p. 100.

[11] Ellul, p. 46.

[12] Ellen G. White, *The Desire of Ages,* pp. 453, 454.

[13] *Ibid.,* p. 454.